SCOTTSBORO UNMASKED

DECATUR'S STORY

PEGGY ALLEN TOWNS

authorHOUSE®

AuthorHouse™
1663 Liberty Drive
Bloomington, IN 47403
www.authorhouse.com
Phone: 1 (800) 839-8640

Published by AuthorHouse 02/16/2018

ISBN: 978-1-5462-2570-6 (sc)
ISBN: 978-1-5462-2569-0 (hc)
ISBN: 978-1-5462-2648-2 (e)

Library of Congress Control Number: 2018901132

Print information available on the last page.

Any people depicted in stock imagery provided by Thinkstock are models, and such images are being used for illustrative purposes only. Certain stock imagery © Thinkstock.

On occasion offensive racial labels are used in this book. Such words reflect the attitudes and principles of our society during that time and are important if we are to unmask our history in its true content. I regret any insult it may cause.

This book is printed on acid-free paper.

In Memory of my Parents

George W. Allen and Myrtle Lyle Allen
and

Dedicated to all those who have the
courage to take a stand for justice.

CONTENTS

"Justice should be dispensed alike to all, to rich and poor, to Northerners and Southerners, to whites and blacks. It should be administered calmly and fairly, without hate, without prejudice, with due regard for the law, the facts and the respect of descent humankind."[1]
Milwaukee Sentinel

"History, despite its wrenching pain, cannot be unlived, but if faced with courage, need not be lived again."
Dr. Maya Angelou

DISCOVER

"…to obtain knowledge of; arrive at through research or study; to learn or reveal; to expose."
Webster Dictionary

ACKNOWLEDGEMENTS

I am indebted to many, but first and foremost, I want to thank God for giving me the insight and courage to honor the voices of those whose stories have to this point been untold or simply forgotten. I am grateful that my parents instilled in us the value of knowing our history. Often my mother would say, "If you don't know where you've been, you'll never know where you're going." Consequently, required reading for all of her children was Dan T. Carter's book, "*Scottsboro. A Tragedy of the American South.*"

A special thanks to my family for their support. My daughter, Latrisha Raquel; grandchildren, Alyssiya, Nickoles, Faith and Alyssia; my siblings, George, Emma, Susie, James, Petrina and Cynthia, cousins Brinda and Donnie: You all encouraged me to tell our story. To my husband, Edward Towns, my laptop is my friend, thank you for understanding. Friends, Malinda Ray, Deborah Robinson, and Dr. Wylheme H. Ragland, you have always been my biggest cheerleaders. Lois, thank you.

I am immensely appreciative of John Allison and the Morgan County Archives staff; pictures do paint a thousand words. Lindy Ashwander and the 2009 "Big Read" program, little did you know that the "Walking

Tour" would spark my consciousness and engage me on this extraordinary journey.

Much gratitude also goes to my writers group; John, Joyce and Judy. You contributed in such a special way and thank you hardly seems enough. Your feedback was immeasurable. You kept me on track and encouraged me when I had writers block. Thank you for the critiques, suggestions, confidence and constant support.

To the many publishers and authors who have told this story, particularly, Dan T. Carter, and James Goodman, your research was invaluable. Dr. Kwando M. Kinshasa, the mention of Tom Brown, took me on an amazing adventure that I would not have otherwise visited. Thank you for your work.

INTRODUCTION

O
rdinary people can have an extraordinary impact on the world. The chilling story of the Scottsboro Boys' trial marked a revolutionizing turning point in our American justice system. On the face of it, the decision to relocate the trial fifty miles away to Decatur, Alabama, did not look like a move that would shake the good ol' boy system of the South, but it did.

In Depression-era Decatur, there were many educated and self-employed blacks. The segregated African American community had its own physicians, dentists, lawyers, realtors, and numerous businesses. These people did not need to concern themselves with fear of economic consequences or repercussions from whites, if they became involved in the trial of black boys accused of raping two white women. Because of their courage to stand up for justice, countless men and women in their small community were inspired to make a difference.

It all began the morning of March 25, 1931, a chilly spring day, when a forty-two car freight train slowly pulled out of Chattanooga, Tennessee. At varying points along the way, black and white drifters had hurriedly scampered onto the rolling cars. As the locomotive trundled into Alabama, a fight broke out among the train-hopping hobos. The blacks overpowered their white challengers, and the whites jumped off the speeding freight.

When the train pulled into Paint Rock, Alabama, nine black youth who would become known as the "Scottsboro Boys," were met by a group of about fifty agitated farmers and townsfolk. Armed with venomous hatred and weapons, the men forced the blacks off the train and hauled them off to a Scottsboro jail without an explanation.

Rape charges were formulated. Reaction to such an accusation, particularly when a white woman accused a black man, often led to an unspeakable violence. Frequently the accused was castrated, tarred and feathered, hanged, or received the death penalty with America's legal lynchings.

Accordingly, the "Scottsboro Nine" had already been convicted, in a trial by race, prejudices and inflammatory articles in southern newspapers. Twelve days later, eight of the young men were sentenced to die in Alabama's electric chair, the "Yellow Mama."[1] Appeals led ultimately to two landmark United States Supreme Court decisions. The International Labor Defense (ILD) hired Walter Pollack to argue the cases to the U.S. Supreme Court. In *Powell vs Alabama,* on November 1932, the highest court in the land concluded that the defendants had been denied adequate counsel. Powell's case was the "first time the Court had reversed a state criminal conviction for violation of a criminal procedural provision of the United States Bill of Rights."[1] The death sentences were set aside.

Later in another ruling, *Norris vs Alabama* (1935), the court came to a decision that the state of Alabama had

---

[1] Yellow Mama is the nickname given to Alabama's electric chair, which was used for executions from 1927-2002.

illegally excluded blacks from their juror rolls, solely because of their race. New trials were awarded based on the judgment that blacks had been "systematically excluded from the petit juries in Jackson County and that by reason of such systematic exclusion of members of the Negro race there were no Negroes on the list of jurors of Morgan County."[2]

Racism continues to throw devastating blows to people of color and understanding our past is critical to our present state, if we are to respond to the many injustices that our society is faced with today. In this work, my search for obscure facts led to fascinating untold stories of Decatur's common citizens, revealing critical information overlooked when most writers tell this story. I applaud the courage of the many brave people, (some whose names are unknown) who rallied together to take a stand against Jim Crow laws and Alabama's racist justice system.

However, despite the heroism of Blacks during the Scottsboro Boys trials, the many years of appeals, rising tensions, and continuous threats were trying on families, and triggered an exodus of black professionals. Dr. Theodore Boalware, a pharmacist, on Bank Street, was threatened and left virtually overnight. He first went to Tennessee and later to Kentucky. Dr. Willis Wood, a dentist, relocated to Montgomery. After several cross burnings on his front lawn, and for fear that his family would be harmed, Dr. Frank Sykes left town in 1937. He returned to Baltimore and started a dental practice there.

Personally, I needed to tell this story for a number of reasons. The Scottsboro Boys Trials have captivated me because my father lived in Jackson County at the time of the arrest. All the trials except the first were held in my hometown, Decatur. My maternal grandmother, Bertha Polk Lyle, attended the trials. Lastly, I write this story because false accusations of rape entrenched with rampant racial discrimination always have had disquieting effects on the community. To name a few dire consequences of blatant racial violence:

- Hangings in the 1903 Bloodsworth case
- A rape allegation involving Thomas Brown that occurred a few months after the Scottsboro trial began in Decatur
- The rape case of Billy Joe
- The 1978 arrest and conviction of Tommy "Brother Tommy" Lee Hines

The most devastating event was the arrest of Tommy Lee Hines, a jovial, 25-year old, mentally challenged black man. He was a student at the Cherry Street School Developmental Center and had an IQ of 35 and the "mental capacity" of a six-year old. Tommy could not read, recite the alphabets, count to ten, nor repeat the days of the week in sequence. Despite these facts, after being held in the Decatur City jail for two and a half days, he was coerced into signing a confession.

Brother Tommy lived with his parents Richard and Bessie Hines. He was short in stature, had dark brown skin, kinky short hair, and wore glasses. Each day the young man made his daily rounds through the neighborhood. He moved with long strides, grinning, and bowing his head, as he greeted people, "Hi y'all doing?"

The black community was outraged with disbelief when Hines was arrested for raping three white women and robbing one of them. The allegation that Tommy was driving a car was ludicrous. He couldn't even ride a bicycle; everyone in the community knew that. Convinced of his innocence, Blacks organized at local churches in a campaign to *"Free Tommy Lee."* Hundreds of concerned citizens came together in protest to fight against this endemic social tyranny, just as they had done during the Scottsboro trials. Marvin B. Dinsmore, a white man, was one of the first to speak out.

Mr. Dinsmore had served as president of The Arc of Morgan County, The Arc of Alabama, and president of the Mental Health Association Board.[2] His daughter and Tommy had attended the North Central Alabama Center for the Developmentally Disabled at the old Cherry Street School. Very much aware of Tommy's mental aptitude, Dinsmore was saddened and appalled at this injustice. He used his personal resources to assist with the legal defense fund and testified on the defendant's behalf: "Most of us knew he was innocent," he said. "Why, Tommy couldn't even put a key in a car door, let alone drive it...the sad thing about it all, everyone knew it. Unfortunately, the real situation got lost in all the hullabaloo."[3]

Protesting the arrest and convictions, blacks held numerous prayer rallies on the city hall and courthouse lawns. The demonstrations attracted the attention of the Ku Klux Klan and barking dogs. They, too, held mass meetings that culminated with fiery cross burnings. It all came to a head May 26, 1979, the day the two sides met. A march had been organized by the Southern Christian

---

[2] The Arc of Alabama organized in 1957 and dedicated to advocating for the rights and needs of children and adults with cognitive, intellectual and developmental disabilities.

Leadership Conference, commemorating the one year anniversary of Hines' arrest. While marching down the streets, Blacks were singing and chanting: *"Free Tommy Lee. Free Tommy Lee. Free Tommy Lee!"* In protest, the Klan had also orchestrated a rally. Approximately one hundred hooded members had gathered. They paraded with a blackened effigy of Tommy Lee Hines that dangled by a noose from the back of a pickup truck. In a maddening attempt to block the street and prevent black marchers from proceeding down Bank Street, the Klan threw the dummy in the street and beat it. Blacks were furious; screaming curses were exchanged by both sides. In a flash, utter chaos broke out. Shots were fired. People were down.

What happened to Tommy Lee Hines as late as 1978 and to the Scottsboro Boys in 1931 dates back to the era of slavery and to Thomas Dixon's 1905 novel, *The Clansman*, from which the silent film *Birth of a Nation* was adapted. Dixon promoted the image of the black man as a brute and sexual predator of white women. It was an ugly, devastating stereotype that persisted. Throughout history, a false perception that black men are inclined to rape white women had always been postulated. Accusations of rape spurred on by white females had resulted in malicious and ruthless arrests and convictions as well as vicious lynchings, all in the name of justice. These tactics were used as a method of control and were meant to intimidate and degrade blacks, to "keep them in their place."

Today, all these years later, racial injustices and intolerances are just as ubiquitous. When will America and the world eradicate the bitter root of racial intolerance that proliferates in our communities like a venomous monster? When will it stop? When will Lady Justice's eyes truly be blind to bigotry and the racial prejudices that still exist today? Only when we as a people open our hearts and eyes to see one another without discrimination can we embrace the sanctity of life and find equal ground.

May God help us all! Amen.

CHAPTER 1

A DISTURBANCE

Vine Street had been relatively quiet. Local residents sat on their front porches chatting with neighbors and a host of casual passersby. Wandering patrons strolled in and out of the mixture of shops and cafés that were purposefully intermingled with houses. Having felt the depression, a few of the stores in the predominantly black community had closed and were now reopened and owned by Syrian families.

Earlier that evening, a group of armed masked men had made a surprise entry into a dance and ordered it shut down. Now a mysterious caravan of automobiles and trucks cruised slowly the well-known thoroughfare. The occupants leaned out the windows, bellowing racist remarks and brandishing pistols, rifles and shotguns. Suddenly, flashes of light and a loud storm of bullets rapidly echoed into the clammy night air. Bystanders ran and ducked for cover, hiding behind bushes and disappearing into nearby dwellings.[1] Almost in the same instant, the vehicles sped off.

Hurling its rider to the ground, a large bicycle tumbled over with a loud, crashing thump. Crimson red blood

1

puddled around the body and quickly saturated the ground. Sixteen-year-old James Royal was dead. A single 16-guage shotgun blast had hit him on the right side of his chest.

Royal had been employed by Carl Arantz Drug Store. His responsibilities included straightening up the store and delivering items using his bicycle. That night, August 21, 1933, his last delivery run was to the home of Dr. Winston H. Sherard, a black physician who lived on Vine Street. After dropping off the medicine, Royal mounted his bike and peddled over to where three of his friends Otis Webb, Frank Brawley and James Eddie were standing, near the corner of Madison and McCartney Streets.[2] Minutes later, James Royal's lifeless body fell to the ground.

As the perpetrators ravaged the community, sporadic violence swirled through the night. Sounds of gunshots broke the silence as a barrage of spraying bullets rattled the Magnolia Drug store, operated by Arthur O. Sheffey on Bank Street.[3] Bricks, irons and bottles were hurled at other shops and businesses and the shattering sounds of breaking glass echoed noisily as windows and inside cases crackled and popped. Fiery crosses spewed bright orange and bluish flames in front of homes and the nearby Church Street bridge overpass.

The air was fierce with the brassy stench of fired gunpowder as outright horror continued into the early morning. In the midst of the pandemonium, the black community quickly responded by setting up guard posts to defend themselves. Dr. Sherard and his sons were among those who armed themselves and took turns keeping watch over the family. The insurgency of violence was frightening. Some days later, a local newspaper reported, because of being terrorized "black churches closed their [doors] in darkness after nightfall."[4] The message resonated loudly throughout the town. The rage that had consumed the night was pumped by another allegation of rape, but this time, in Decatur.

CHAPTER 2

DECATUR, ALABAMA

O nce the home of Cherokee Indians, Decatur, was named in honor of naval hero Stephen Decatur who was a hero of the Barbary Wars, and the War of 1812. Formerly called Rhodes Ferry, the settlement became known as Decatur around 1820. During the War of Rebellion, commonly known as the Civil War, the town served as a strategic point because of its location on the Tennessee River and on account of the railroad. Mainly occupied by Federal troops during the war, it was also the first of two Alabama towns to organize a regiment of "African American" soldiers known as the 106th United States Colored Infantry.

During the Great Depression, the town was hard hit. The L&N Railroad Shop had closed, as had textile mills and other small factories in town.

On March 27, 1933, the trial of the century opened at Decatur. A few months earlier, Southern lawyer George Chamlee had successfully won a change of venue for the nine boys accused of rape, not to Birmingham, Alabama, where he thought the alleged perpetrators might have a better chance of getting a fair trial, but to this river city.

Chamlee, an International Labor Defense (ILD) attorney, was a stocky man who had practiced law for forty years in Tennessee.[3] A former district attorney in Hamilton County, he was known to take on challenging and difficult cases. Chamlee's father had owned slaves and he had served in the Confederate army during the Civil War.

The first order of business for lead counsel, Samuel Leibowitz, was to move to quash the March 1931 indictments and quash the venire on grounds of the continuous omission of African-Americans. The ILD had made a humanitarian appeal to the New York attorney, asking that he take the case under the conditions that he would not be paid or reimbursed for expenses.[1] He accepted.

The son of Isaac and Bina Lebeau, Leibowitz was born in Romania. His family immigrated to the United States when he was four years old and made their home in New York. To improve business opportunities, his father was encouraged to Americanize their Jewish name from Lebeau to Leibowitz. Graduating from Jamaica High School in Queens, New York, Samuel worked his way through college and law school at Cornell University, where he received a law degree in 1916. Successfully defending notorious criminals like Al Capone, he gained an extraordinary reputation as a criminal defense attorney.[2]

Accompanying a slender and balding Leibowitz to Decatur were Joseph Brodsky and George Chamlee. Brodsky, a New York lawyer, was the chief legal counsel

---

[3] The International Labor Defense (ILD) was the legal advocacy branch in the United States that included communist as well as others. It was formed in 1925 to counter groups like the Ku Klux Klan.

with the ILD. The Scottsboro Boys legal team was expanded when a sharp, prominent lawyer from Decatur, Thomas Clifton "T. C." Almon joined them. Almon would later serve as the city's attorney from 1935 to 1938. Afterwards, while working in Governor Bibb Graves' administration, he was appointed Probate Judge in Morgan County, a position he served in for thirty years.

In preparation for the alleged offenders' defense, the clever team journeyed across the railroad tracks. In the South, the tracks almost always signified a distinct color line that segregated the mostly black neighborhood from the predominantly white one. Although blacks primarily occupied three separate parts of town, the majority of them lived on the northwest side of the tracks in Old Town. This neighborhood was the oldest in the city. It was founded in 1821, a few years before the Alabama Legislature incorporated the City of Decatur, in 1826. Old Town was unique because the majority of the town's most powerful and influential black citizens lived here. Attesting to this fact were their large opulent homes with distinctive architectural designs and ornamental wrought iron fences. Similarly, the majority of minority owned businesses and nearly all the black churches were located in this community.

Like most southern towns during the Jim Crow era, Decatur was regulated by sanctioned and unwritten–but clearly understood – laws.[4] For example, if a black and white person met on a sidewalk, the black person had to

---

[4] The Jim Crow laws were racial segregation state and local laws enacted after Reconstruction in the South. Jim Crow laws mandated segregation of public schools, public places and public transportation, and the segregation of restrooms, restaurants and drinking fountains for whites and blacks. The U.S. military was also segregated, as were federal workplaces.

step off. When addressing whites, one had to say, "yes ma'am" and "no ma'am" and "yes sir" and "no sir." Often, blacks, no matter their age, were referred to by their first name, or insulting and derogatory labels such as "boy" or "gal," "uncle" or "auntie," including other offensive terms. Likewise, blacks understood they were not to make eye contact when speaking to a white person. If one dared to violate this accepted way of life, they could be fired, beaten, jailed or even killed.

Prepared to challenge Alabama's "unwritten law," by which Blacks were undeniably excluded from the jury rolls, the ILD attorneys initiated a dialogue with locals. Gathering plausible evidence to prove their case, they met at various churches with clergy and congregants who did not fear retaliation. One such meeting place was the Baptist Church on Vine Street. Its congregation organized in 1866, just one year after the civil war. The edifice, now known as First Baptist, was designed by the country's second and Alabama's first black, licensed architect, Wallace A. Rayfield. Construction of the church was completed in 1921.

CHAPTER 3

DOOMED

Two years earlier, on March 25, 1931, Deputy Sheriff Charlie Latham and an enraged mob of deputized townsfolk congregated at Paint Rock, Alabama. Sheriff Matthew (M. L.) Wann gave strict orders. "You must capture every Negro on the train and bring them to Scottsboro." He added, "I'm giving you authority to deputize every man you can."[1] A posse of about fifty white men, mostly farmers, stood on each side of the railroad tracks. Their thundering voices rumbled hostile threats as they waited armed and ready to use their shotguns, rifles, pistols, clubs, and other weapons.

Already behind schedule, the southern freight leaving Chattanooga and bound for Memphis pulled out. As the train picked up speed, several hoboes found their "catchout" spots and hopped on at varying intervals. Traveling through Lookout Mountain, the laid-back drifters welcomed the cool but bright, sunny day.

Not long after the iron horse crossed into Alabama near Stevenson, a fight abruptly broke out between the white and black hoboes. One of the white vagrants stepped on Haywood Patterson's hand for a second time. "The next time you want by, just tell me you want by and I let you by," Patterson said.

"Nigger, I don't ask you when I want by," the white man blasted. "What you doing on this train anyway? Nigger bastard, this is a white man's train. You better get off. All you black bastards better get off."[2]

When the train slowed down long enough, the whites jumped off, picked up rocks and began throwing them at the blacks. As soon as they hopped back on, the train, there was a scuffle. The blacks won the fight. All the whites vaulted off the moving train, except one. While Orville Gilley's body dangled unsteadily over the side of the train, he was pulled back onto the now fast, rolling cars.[5]

Boiling with outrage, ashamed and defeated, the ejected white men went swiftly to a nearby store at Stevenson to report the fight. Their white skin was pale from a lack of summer sun. They wore shabby clothes, old jackets, tattered pants, and loose-fitting sweaters with layers of long-sleeved shirts underneath. A thread of blood trickled down the face of one of them. Agitated, the group of men told Arthur Woodall, the storekeeper who was also a part-time deputy, that they had been beaten and thrown off the train. Immediately, Woodall contacted the Sheriff, who called ahead to stop the train at Scottsboro. Just minutes earlier, the Memphis-bound convoy had rushed by.

At Paint Rock, the steel cars jerked and came to a shrieking halt. Swarming the train, the search party rummaged through every car. One by one, the posse soon apprehended nine black youth who were scattered

---

[5] State of Alabama Jackson County Indictment, April 7, 1931. The names of the white boys were John Gleason, John Ferguson, Roy Thurman, Lindsey and Odell Gladwell, Lester Carter and Orville Gilley.

throughout the train in different cars. Some of them were dressed in well-worn bibbed overalls, multiple shirts, and loose-fitting, frayed jackets. Others wore old, threadbare pants and shirts topped with baggy, heavy wool sweaters to keep warm on the cool spring days. All the youth sported caps or wide-brimmed hats. Ragged and disheveled, their brown skin, ranging from light tan to dark brown, glistened with fear, as they were tied together with plow line, herded onto the back of a wobbly old flatbed truck, and hauled away to the Jackson County jail at Scottsboro.

In addition to the nine blacks, three whites were also pulled off the train. A shocking truth was exposed when two of them, dressed in lightly soiled overcoats, faded worn-out overalls, and sporting caps, happened to be women. The pair, Victoria Price and Ruby Bates, had also jumped the train in Chattanooga, Tennessee, and was returning home to Huntsville, Alabama.

When the truck crammed with the black detainees pulled off, Ruby Bates went to Sheriff Charlie Latham and reported that she and her companion had been violently assaulted by the blacks on the train. The women gave all the horrific details without batting an eye. They told Latham how twelve blacks threatened them with a knife and brutally attacked and raped them. The dreadful incident had happened soon after the whites were thrown off the train, as it left Stevenson, the women claimed. Price further stated that Roy Thurman "fought desperately" until he was ordered off the speeding freight train and jumped. Finishing her story, she blurted, "The negroes stopped bothering us about five minutes before the train got to Paint Rock, Alabama, where the men took them off. I fainted shortly after the train stopped."[3]

What was the crime? Had they been savagely hurled into jail because of the fight? The "Scottsboro Boys" or "Scottsboro Nine," as they would become known soon found out that they were arrested for "shooting with intent to murder." One of the white hobos, Roy Thurman, of Jamestown, Virginia, made the charge, stating that the blacks had fired at him five times before he jumped from the speeding train, reported *The Alabama Courier*.[4] Later, the nine youth were charged with rape.

Ranging from ages 12 to 19, four of the black youth knew one another and all had hopped the train at Chattanooga, Tennessee. Two of them were brothers James "Andy" and Leroy "Roy" Wright. Andy, who celebrated his 19th birthday shortly after being arrested, had been a good student. When his father died, he was forced to quit school to help support the family. For several years, he worked as a truck driver for B. L. Tally Produce Company, in Chattanooga, Tennessee.[5] Accompanying his elder brother was twelve-year-old Roy, the youngest of the youth arrested. It was the juvenile's first experience riding the rails with hoboes.

The other two youth acquainted with the Wright brothers were Haywood Patterson and Eugene Williams. Born in Elberton, Georgia, on December 12, 1913, Haywood left school after the third grade and later worked as a delivery boy. He had been hoboing trains since he was age fourteen.[6]

Eugene Williams, thirteen years old, was the second youngest to be taken into custody that day. He was described by *Life Magazine's* July 1937 edition as a "sullen, shifty mulatto." He had been employed as a dishwasher for a while at Dixie Café in Chattanooga. All of the youth anticipated finding work in Memphis.

As fate would have it, five other blacks arrested that day had also hopped a ride on the Memphis bound freight – Olen Montgomery, Clarence Norris, Ozie Powell, Willie Roberson, and Charles Weems.

Olen Montgomery, a native of Monroe, Georgia, was totally blind in his left eye and had only 10 percent vision in the other. At the time of his arrest, he was traveling to Memphis in hope of getting badly needed glasses. Montgomery rode along in a tank car on the southern freight train.[7] After obtaining glasses in prison, he would later write letters on behalf of the others.[8]

Clarence Norris, son of a sharecropper, was from Molina, Georgia. When he was seven years old, he began working in the fields, and was later employed as an assistant for a stonemason. Norris took to the rails at age nineteen. Although his clothes showed signs of wear, he was neatly dressed. His processed hair was slicked down to his head. When he was pulled off the train at Paint Rock, he was on his way to Sheffield, Alabama, to live with an aunt.[9]

With only a first grade education, Ozie Powell worked in local mills as a youngster. At age fourteen, he left his home near Atlanta and hopped the Chattanooga-Memphis freight train. He knew none of the others who were indicted with him when he jumped on a cross-tie car, as they pulled out of Chattanooga.[10]

Willie Roberson was born on the Fourth of July, 1915, near Columbus, Georgia. At the time of his arrest his mental age was nine. With a severe case of syphilis and gonorrhea, he badly needed medical treatment, and was bumming a ride to a Memphis hospital.[11] Very frail, his private parts were swollen and covered with lesions, and his legs were so weak that he could hardly walk without the aid of a cane. Roberson said he was in so much pain that he barely made it onto a car near the end of the train and that he laid down for most of the journey.

Charles Weems was the oldest and had once worked as a delivery boy at Watson's Drug Store in Atlanta. His mother passed when he was four-years old. Weems and Haywood Patterson were involved in the fight that broke out in the gondola.[6] Little did any of the Scottsboro Nine realize that this train ride would invariably unite them together, forever.

Both Victoria Price, twenty one, and Ruby Bates, seventeen; lived in rundown shacks with their mothers in a dilapidated and racially mixed section of northern Huntsville. Considered to be "poor white trash," the two were said to have "loose character, slept in box cars …and associated with Negroes"[12] Price who had been married twice, was from Fayetteville, Tennessee. She often used the alias name, Victoria McClendon.

Ruby Bates was born in the Eva, Alabama community, and moved to Huntsville a few years before the arrest at Paint Rock. The young woman who dipped snuff, worked at the Margaret Cotton mill. Said to be the quieter of the two, her family was the only white family in the block of the predominately black area on Depot Street.[13] The two women were known for their sexual promiscuity.

The black youth denied any charges of rape and when Clarence Norris called the women liars, a guard immediately swung at him with his bayonet and said. "Nigger, you know damn well how to talk to white

---

[6] Gondola is an open-topped rail car used for transporting loose bulk materials.

women."[14] In a split second, he raised his hand for protection, just as the sharp blade slashed his finger to the bone.

All over Jackson and adjoining counties, people were overwhelmed with emotions. Throughout the day, anxious hate-filled crowds came from all directions. By sundown, the angry agitators numbering about three hundred circled the jail with guns, poles, ropes and other makeshift weapons. They were egged on by jeering vicious remarks, and demanded, "Bring them niggers outta there. If you don't bring them out, we'll come in and get 'em."[15] The Alabama National Guard was deployed to assist the sheriff in protecting the prisoners. Guardsmen brandishing machine guns and rifles with razor-edged bayonets at the end, kept the masses at bay. The next day, the nine prisoners were transported to a Gadsden jail, as a precautionary measure.

Judge Alfred E. Hawkins, of the Ninth Judicial Circuit Court, ordered all members of the Alabama bar to represent the defendants, but none accepted. On March 30, Steven Roddy, a lawyer from Chattanooga, Tennessee, arrived early to attend the Grand Jury hearing at the Jackson County Courthouse.[16] After meeting with the Interdenominational Colored Ministers Alliance, he had been retained for $120 to represent the defendants. A real-estate attorney, Roddy often took on cases for blacks in Chattanooga, which required very little preparation. He drank heavily and had spent time in an asylum, for alcohol-related mental disorders.[17]

The trials were rushed through in record breaking time. On April 6, twelve days from the arrest, members of the 167th Infantry of the National Guard brought the prisoners back to Scottsboro, the county seat, to stand trial. The first Monday was also known as "Horse Swapper's Day." A sea of vendors spread their goods all around the town's square. Tent shows provided entertainment. Merchandise was bought and sold. Bands played. People were energetic. Besides the normal crowd, thousands of others gathered at Scottsboro. The town was consumed in a carnival atmosphere. Many of the men were armed and had been stirred up by the rape allegations and upcoming trials.

When court opened at 8:30 that morning, excited spectators assembled, many spurred with a lynch spirit. Around the courthouse, the immediate vicinity bore a close resemblance of a war zone. Standardized brown military-issued uniforms, combat boots and wide brimmed ranger-looking hats distinguished the armed troops who kept the hostile crowd orderly. Only people who possessed a special permit were admitted inside the courthouse.[18]

In court, the parents saw their sons for the first time since they had been arrested. They had attempted to visit them while they were in custody but were turned away. Under the influence, Steven Roddy staggered into the courtroom. According to an onlooker, "He was so stewed, he could scarcely walk straight."[19] The threatening crowd cursed and bellowed all sorts of obscenities at him. Wrestling with how the community would perceive him for representing the defendants, he complained to the presiding judge and refused to admit that he was the defendants' attorney. Later, he asked not to be recorded as defense counsel. Scottsboro attorney, Miles A. "Milo" Moody stepped up and agreed to assist him.[20] A former

Alabama legislator, at nearly seventy years old, he suffered from senility.

As court convened, the defense immediately requested a change of venue, referring to the widespread prejudice in newspapers and that of the townsfolk. Hawkins overruled the motion. The suspects were tried in four separate cases.

The alleged offenders' attorney was unprepared to defend them. Clarence Norris would later recall that they had not seen Roddy until the day of the trial, when they were carried to a side room in the courthouse where he informed them that he was their legal counsel. Despite their plea of innocence, Roddy urged his clients: "It was possible to save some of your lives if you plead guilty to all charges."[21]

Over and over again, Victoria Price gave her theatrical account of the alleged incident. She told how they had found work and was returning home to get their belongings when: "A whole bunch of Negroes suddenly jumped into the gondola, two of them shooting pistols and the others showing knives."[22] During her testimony, she maintained that all nine of the defendants held knives at their throats, pinned down their legs, tore off their clothes, and brutally raped them.[23]

Other witnesses for the state, Drs. Robert R. Bridges and Marvin Lynch, gave their expert opinions. The two examined the women shortly after Ruby Bates, who was the initial accuser, said they were raped. Five other witnesses were called to support the supposed victims' claim. Roddy made very little effort to provide evidence that might help his clients avoid the death penalty. Each of the defendants was called to testify.

One by one the all-white jury delivered its four

verdicts - "guilty." At the news, the crowd cheered uncontrollably and grew louder and louder. A band played "There'll be a Hot Time in the Old Town Tonight."[24] On April 9, 1931, Judge Alfred E. Hawkins, handed down eight death sentences. Condemned to die in the electric chair at Kilby prison on Friday, July 10, 1931, were: Charlie Weems, and Ozie Powell both of Atlanta; Eugene Williams, Andy Wright, Clarence Norris, and Haywood Patterson, all of Chattanooga; Olen Montgomery, Monroe, Georgia, and Willie Roberson, of Columbus, Georgia.[25]

The verdict for Roy Wright ended in a mistrial because he was so young. The hung jury was split on his sentence-seven for the death penalty by electrocution and five for life in prison.[26] This typical act of white Southern justice may have sounded reasonable for the crime, except for one thing. Maintaining their innocence, all of the defendants plead *not guilty*.

CHAPTER 4

DISREGARDED

Was there a possibility that these nine black youth could receive a fair and impartial trial in the South? On March 27, 1933, two years after the first convictions in Scottsboro, time for the appeals had come. The case had gone all the way to the United States Supreme Court which ruled on November 7, 1932 in *Powell vs Alabama*. The landmark decision acknowledged that equal protection given under the Fourteenth Amendment of the Constitution had been denied during the Scottsboro trials.[7] Specifically, in a capital trial, all citizens should have the right to adequate legal representation.

Outside the Morgan County Courthouse in Decatur, Alabama, a beautiful crisp, sunny spring day greeted

---

[7] Section 1. All persons born or naturalized in the United States and subject to the jurisdiction thereof, are citizens of the United States and of the State wherein they reside. No State shall make or enforce any law which shall abridge the privileges or immunities of citizens of the United States; nor shall any State deprive any person of life, liberty, or property, without due process of law; nor deny to any person within its jurisdiction the equal protection of the laws. (http://www.14thamendment.us/amendment/14th_amendment.html)

inquisitive watchers. Two massive statues, Lady Justice and a Confederate soldier, set amidst looming oak trees. John Evans, the janitor brandishing a broom and wearing faded overalls, put the finishing touches on the Courthouse. He made sure every inch was spic and span. Additional parking spaces had already been marked off for the anticipated crowd.

The judge presiding over the retrials was James E. Horton, Jr. Soft-spoken, dark graying hair, slender built and over six feet tall, Horton had earned a reputation for honesty. Some said he resembled President Abraham Lincoln without a beard. Born in Limestone County, he was the son of a probate judge and Southern planter who once owned slaves. James Jr. studied medicine for a short time at Vanderbilt and a while later, in 1899, received a Bachelor of Laws degree from Cumberland University, in Lebanon, Tennessee. Horton served for a while in both the Alabama legislature and the State Senate. Later, in 1922, he was elected judge of the Eighth Circuit Court.[1]

A massive crowd of more than 2000 curious spectators thronged the courthouse grounds – men and women of all ages, educational levels, races, and socio-economic classes. Most of the Southern-bred men were decked out in bibbed caps, dungarees and overalls while others wore their Sunday best. Much of the time was spent talking to one another, as they waited for the trials to begin. Some of them chewed on homemade toothpicks carved from small twigs, others sported wads of chewing tobacco tucked away in their jaws or snuff lumped in their bottom lips. Rivulets of brown juice oozed out the corners of their mouths or drizzled down their chins. Assorted clusters of people were sprawled over the property like blankets of patchwork quilts. Throughout the course of the day, the onlookers basked in the sun and feasted from grease-stained brown paper bags, shoe boxes, picnic baskets, or molasses buckets.

People also lined the quiet nearby streets surrounding the courthouse. All anticipated what many later called "the trial of the century" and hoped to catch a glimpse of the alleged rapists. A pamphlet the "Unpublished Inside Story of the Infamous Scottsboro Case," written by J. Glenn Jordan was being circulated to incite further racial discrimination, hatred and violence.

While waiting for the retrial in Decatur, seven of the nine convicted offenders were transferred from death row at Kilby prison in Montgomery to the jail in Birmingham. Captain Joseph Burleson and thirty members of the Alabama National Guard, Company C, Engineers, from Hartselle, Alabama, had been activated for guard duty.[2] Morgan County's local sheriff, Albert W. "Bud" Davis, made his position clear that they were there not so much as to protect the prisoners but rather to prevent them from escaping.[3] A native of Falkville, Alabama, Davis succeeded his father Benjamin Ethan Davis, as sheriff in 1930.

After several hours, around two o'clock that afternoon, a convoy of cars rushed onto the courthouse lawn where the guardsmen were waiting. Carrying machine guns, deputies abruptly jumped out of their vehicles and ordered the prisoners to unload. The alleged criminals were escorted inside the courthouse, dressed in prison-issued blue denim overalls and shackled in pairs. A verdict other than that of guilty and a sentence of anything less than burning in the electric chair would be received by the gathering mob with hostility, potentially leading to physical harm or even death for the prisoners.

Inside the two-story yellow brick building, intense anger produced an atmosphere of resentment for some and fear for others. Explosive accounts of the atrocious rape case attracted worldwide attention. The segregated second-floor courtroom was dimly lit. Aging, pale yellowed shades covered the windows, concealing much of the morning and afternoon sunlight. Suspended from long stemmed rods, the schoolhouse light fixtures hazily illuminated the chamber. Large fans hanging from the ceiling spun noisily to provide a gentle breeze, rousing the stifling air. Occasionally, the wooden floors squeaked when walked upon. Around the room, the sound of spick, spick, spick, echoed as tobacco chewers and snuff dippers, (who seemed to be competing) took their aim at the shiny brass spittoons adorning the floor. A light grayish smoke left by cigarette and cigar smokers hung over the room.

Excited spectators settled into the packed room that was filled to capacity. The seats went quickly, as Sheriff Bud Davis' "first come, first served," policy was strictly enforced. Of the 425 seats, one section was reserved for blacks, four for whites, and one side for both blacks and whites. Outside the expansive wooden double doors with transoms, the long hallway was jammed packed with people who had been standing for hours. Eager to get a look inside the room, their necks strained and stretched to catch a glimpse. Bathrooms and water fountains marked "colored" (black) and "white" were representative of the inescapable practices of the Jim Crow South and further established separation among the races.

Dozens of visiting news reporters from all over the

country had been assigned seats in the makeshift press boxes. Journalists arriving late scrambled to get inside the overflowing courtroom. Thomas M. Davenport was assigned to cover the stories for both The Associated Press and the local newspaper, *The Decatur Daily*. Fearing blacks would not be permitted inside the courtroom; The Associated Negro Press hired John Spivak, a white reporter. Another news writer, Raymond Daniell wrote for *The New York Times*. Two black correspondents sat together. William N. Jones, Managing Editor of *The Afro American* and Plummer [P] Bernard Young, Managing Editor of *The Norfolk Journal and Guide*, were the only black journalists assigned press passes. Near the section reserved for blacks, a small table was set up for them on the opposite side from the white journalists. According to *The Afro American*, their reporters "found a stopping place in the home of an old Decatur family...in a white neighborhood, just a few doors from where Victoria Price was living."

At the opening of court, the hope of the defense was centered on their argument to quash the indictments of the accused. As soon as the charges were read, Leibowitz, the chief defense attorney, expressed his "faith in the fairness of the God-fearing people of Decatur and Morgan County."[4] He then made a motion to repeal the charges on the grounds that no members of the defendants' race sat on the grand jury that convicted the blacks in Jackson County, therefore, the constitutional rights of the alleged attackers had been denied. Prosecutor and State Attorney General Thomas Knight, Jr, vehemently denied the allegations.

A native of Greensboro, Alabama, and a veteran of World War I, at thirty-four years old Knight had been elected the youngest attorney general in the history of

Alabama. Aiding him in prosecuting the Scottsboro case in Decatur were: Thomas S. Lawson, assistant attorney general; Wade Wright, Morgan County solicitor; and Harle (H. G.) Bailey, prosecutor in the first trials at Scottsboro.[5] During the proceedings, Knight was insensitive, insulting and sometimes even a ruthless cross-examiner. Reporters nevertheless thought he was "likeable."

His father, Thomas Knight, Sr., had been one of the justices on the Alabama Supreme Court who wrote the opinion that Jackson County was undeniably fair in their indictment and conviction during the first Scottsboro trial. The Elder Knight had said, "The people seem to have conducted themselves with a commendable spirit and desire to let the law take its due course."[6]

Leibowitz was determined to establish that only the names of white males were logged on the jury rolls that sentenced the Scottsboro boys to death. He hoped to demonstrate that "negroes were consistently and systematically excluded from the juries of Jackson County."[7] In a strategic move, he made a request to examine the county's venire list. Surprisingly, over the strong objection of the prosecuting attorney, the judge granted his request to view Jackson County's secret jury roster.

Public sentiment against the Scottsboro Boys was so strong that an article appeared in the *Jackson County Sentinel* two years earlier declaring:

> After we forget the rope to pick up "the code" for the safety and benefit of the negroes, we are told that we must have negro jurors on any jury trying the blacks if they are to get "their rights"...A negro jury would be a curiosity–and some curiosities are embalmed–you know.[8]

The statement was a two-fold reminder and chilling warning that the white citizens had not taken the law into their own hands but allowed "the code" (court-laws governing people) to determine the fate of the Scottsboro Boys. The editorial was also a threat to the safety and well-being of any black who would serve on a jury.

For little more than a day and a half, Haywood Patterson's attorney questioned witnesses, who examined the list from which the jurors were drawn in the first trials. At first, white men who were familiar with the jury system in Jackson County took the stand. Bursting with an air of arrogance, they made condescending and ridiculing remarks. When James Stockton Benson, editor of a local weekly newspaper, *The Progressive Age,* was asked if he knew any blacks who possessed the qualifications according to the statute, he responded with an attack on their integrity. "I think they wouldn't have the character. I mean they wouldn't be honest. They will nearly all steal...I wouldn't exclude any of them [from stealing]."[9] The courtroom responded in mockery, bursting into laughter. Judge Horton pounded his gavel to quiet the spectators. But then Benson noted that Mark Taylor, owner of a local dry cleaner, possessed a good reputation and could read and write. "He speaks pretty intelligently for a negro. You can tell the difference in the way they talk."[10]

Next, Jeff E. Moody, president of the Jury Board, mounted the witness stand. Looking him straight in the eyes, the lead defense counsel pressed him firmly about the all-white jury pool that convicted the nine young men during the initial trial. Moody answered that he had nothing to do with the selection process, since he was only elected in 1932. Leibowitz animatedly asked him to recite the law regarding juror qualifications, he answered: "Well a man has to have good character…good judgment, intelligent, honest, and not afflicted with disease."

"Diseased?" Patterson's attorney asked. "No man is disqualified because he is diseased if his disease isn't permanent and [does not]…affect his mentality, is that something new to you?"[11]

An increasingly tense war of words erupted between the state prosecutor and the defense counsel. Caught in the crossfire was Moody, who was finally permitted to reveal his limited understanding of jury selection qualifications in the county.

Testifying next was J. H. Stewart. He had been a member of the 1930 jury commission that habitually ignored placing the names of qualified blacks on the jury list. When asked if he excluded blacks because they were not qualified, he brazenly announced, "I never took the trouble to find out if there were some intelligent, decent, honest men, when I compiled the roll…I don't know of any other man who took the trouble…to go into the Negro community to find any fit for jury duty."[12]

One more witness, Kelly Morgan, was called for the day. He had been clerk of the Jury Board in 1930. After elaborating on the jury selection process, he concluded as the others, "I cannot name any human being on the face of God's green earth that can tell whether there were any negroes [Negroes] in that jury box."

Under redirect, Leibowitz asked, "Just taking for granted it wasn't, if a man was a negro he was out?"

"We didn't take things for granted," Morgan answered.[13]

Leibowitz's team continued to launch a clever and dangerous campaign to prove that blacks were clearly absent from Jackson County rolls, solely because of skin color.

In a risky move, ten fearless blacks, first one, then the next and the next stepped into the witness box. They had not been subpoenaed.[14] For blacks to testify against a white person was sometimes deadly. Fifty-year-old John Sanford, a lifelong resident of Jackson County, a plasterer by profession and a member of the Joyce Chapel Methodist Episcopal Church, was the first to testify. The dark suit he wore was not new but neatly pressed and fitted his medium frame as if it was tailored. Sanford was a family man and said he often read *The Chattanooga Times* and *The Progressive Age*. He had never been convicted of any crime or offense involving moral turpitude. Furthermore, Sanford said that he often associated with both "white and colored" people in the community. He stated that he had never been called to perform jury duties nor did he know of "any negro in Jackson County" who had been summoned, other than the Federal courts.[15] Leibowitz then asked him about the names of highly regarded black citizens in the county. Sanford acknowledged those he knew, some who attended church with him. He also identified those who he felt demonstrated all the criteria to serve as jurors.[8]

The state attorney general was maliciously hostile and clearly mocking and intimidating to the witness. During cross-examination, Knight stood extremely close, within spitting distance of the witness. Speaking with a piercing

---

[8] Mark Taylor, Hugh Sanford, John Staples, Floyd Snodgrass, P. Toliver, Will Watkins, M. T. Talley, Mr. Rudder, Ed Reed, John Branch, Timberlake, K. D. Snodgrass Dave Stevenson, Bud Moore, C.S. Finley, Travis Mosley, Pleas Larkin, Elijah Matthews, Henry Ross. (Norris vs State of Alabama. United States Supreme Court 1934. Transcript of Record 1934, 120-122)

voice, he pointed his pencil toward the deponent's face: "Tell me what does the word *esteem* means?"

Sanford's deep seated eyes widened. His voice cracked. "I don't know whether I could tell you that or not," he responded.

Infuriated, Leibowitz vaulted from his seat and snapped. "You are not going to bully this witness, or any other witness."

An angry interchange of words continued. When the chief defense counsel eyed the judge, Horton directed him to make his objection to the court. Leibowitz snorted, "Ask the Attorney General to stand back a little bit, and just lower his voice, and stop sticking his fingers in the people's eyes."

Continuing to cross, Knight asked, "And you don't know what the word *esteemed* means, John?"

"Call him Mister," demanded the defendant's lead attorney.

Boiling over with rage, Knight replied angrily. "I am not in the habit of doing that!"[16]

These accepted and visible reminders of the Jim Crow South loomed all through the court proceedings. The *Afro American* newspaper printed that Southern white gentlemen almost always referred to blacks as "nigger" or "nigra."[17]

The next person to take the stand was Cas "C. S." Finley. (Often blacks used initials so that whites would be forced to address them respectfully, using the title Mister, Miss or Misses.) Finley lived in Jackson County all his life. A former school board member, (elected only by the black community for the black schools) he testified that he had never seen a colored man sitting on a jury in Jackson County, nor had he himself served in that capacity. Finley went on to provide the names of those he believed met the requirements to serve as jurors. During cross-examination, Knight almost bickered with his witness, thwarting him about his knowledge of drawing a jury. "I expect to show the absolute ignorance of this negro," he said. Following numerous objections that were overruled, Finley finished his testimony: "I know lots of them (whites) are not competent to be on the jury, and lots of colored people are not competent (too.)"[18]

The defense presumed that sufficient evidence had been offered to show that the Jackson County jury rolls contained no African American residents. Protesting, Knight objected and argued that many whites were not on the rolls either. Inconceivably, Leibowitz asked for the court's indulgence and threatened to bring every man on the list to testify, even if it took twenty five years to do so. The Attorney General was unyielding.

Eight other blacks deemed to be esteemed and of good character corroborated the integrity of those considered to be well-regarded Jackson County citizens. Mark Taylor, school board member and dry cleaner operator, swore under cross-examination that he did not know whether the names defense attorney, George Chamlee, read were on the jury rolls of Jackson County. Travis Mosley, a family man, and landowner who worked on the railroad attested that all the men he was asked about were of good character and sound judgement. Stevenson resident, Lewis (L.C.) Cole, a railroad night watchman agreed. When asked about certain citizens in his neighborhood, he said that they were all of good standing, yet none had ever served on a Circuit Court jury there. Pleas Larkin, a miller at a local grist mill and Larkinsville native, admitted that he had never been called to even come to court as a juror. John Stapler, a resident of Scottsboro since 1896, commented that he often attended trials and in the last thirty years, had never seen a Negro on a jury (Jackson County) in his lifetime. Will Watkins, a 66 year old, lived at Fackler all his life. He too, testified to the names of men, believed to possess the criteria to serve as jurymen. The last to take the stand was Louis (L. C.) Stapler of Limrock. He agreed with the others, saying that in the last thirty years, he had never seen a black man on a jury.[19]

Further proof was presented when Chamlee provided affidavits from other Jackson County citizens affirming that blacks were purposefully left off juries. Mr. F. A. Patterson, former resident of Jackson County, said that for nearly sixty years, he had been familiar with the county's selection process of grand and trial juries: "...a system of Government has been adopted and operated by officials... so that negroes were excluded...practically ever since the end of the Civil War when the negroes were emancipated." Similarly, Rev. W. C. Crutcher, who pastored St. Elizabeth church in Scottsboro for twenty-eight years, also named individuals he believed qualified to be jurors.[9]

All the black witnesses concurred that there were competent black men in the county to serve on juries. Men, who were esteemed, law abiding, good citizens with sound judgment, and without mental defect.

---

[9] Rev. W. C. Crutcher testified that he believed the following blacks were qualified to be jurors: John Sanford, Mark Taylor, L. C. Stapler, K. D. Snodgrass, P. Toliver, M. F. Timberlake, Cam Rudder, Hugh Collier, A Joseph, Louis Cole, Ed Redd and John Branch. (Ebooks Library Cornell University n.d., 51)

Added to the State's questionable evidence was the reality that the names of six African Americans had now been written in, below or on a red line, which indicated fraudulent add-ons to the list. Knight insisted that it was irrelevant that one roll would prove that "negroes were consistently and systematically excluded from the juries of Jackson County."[20]

Just as the State was ready to continue its argument (that blacks had not been let (left) off Jackson County's "true bill" because of their race), without warning, Judge Horton sternly announced: "The motion to quash is overruled." Court recessed until Thursday.

CHAPTER 5

DULY QUALIFIED

An armed posse marched the eight prisoners into the Morgan County jail. The old dilapidated building was in a wretched condition. Two years earlier, the jail had been ruled uninhabitable for white prisoners, who were taken to Huntsville. The air reeked with a putrid, sickening stench of urine, feces, dead decayed animals, and mold. An intrusion of giant rats ran freely and had no fear of humans. Flies, cockroaches and other crawling creatures wandered easily from cell to cell. The old smelly, dirty mattresses were alive with bed bugs that welcomed each of its visitors. "The bed bugs, they're the worst, they get in our clothes and we got no change, just this prison suit," said Andy Wright.[1]

At night, bright lights that were strung craftily outside the jail, cast ghostly figures that glided silently from wall to wall. Just feet away, the hangman's gallows stood as a colossal tower. The thirteen cold gray steel steps led up to the trap door, serving as a constant reminder that there could be a deadly end for the prisoners.[2]

The next morning, Leibowitz, Chamlee and others on his team canvassed the Old Town community, looking for suitable blacks who could serve on Morgan County's juries. They met with the Interdenominational Ministerial Alliance and leading members of the black community. Together they strategized ways to change Alabama's jury systems. First, they selected well-respected and well-educated men to testify. Included on the list were doctors, business owners, pastors, principals and undertakers. Secondly, four lists would be compiled with names of individuals in the county, fit to serve in the jury pools. Thirdly, to be certain there would be a large black presence in the courtroom; locals would be encouraged to attend the trials.

The sight of these white attorneys in Old Town left regulars who congregated at Cornwell restaurant speculating. They talked among themselves about the events and wondered who would come forward to testify against Alabama's illegal and discriminatory practices. Would there be a backlash? Known for its barbecue, the café was one of the most popular eating establishments on Vine Street. It was also the place where Jones and Young, (black reporters) often dined. Special items of buttermilk and grapefruit had been included on the menu exclusively for the journalists, according to Jones' account in *The Afro American*.

The black newspaper also noted that a spy network formed in the African American community. The black informants attended church services and other meetings. They observed and queried the black reporters about possible ILD and communist connections in Decatur and reported back to the white community.[3]

As the pre-trial continued, the new strategy would be similar to that of Jackson County – to overturn the motion to quash the indictment because jury rolls in Morgan County showed a practice of race discrimination. "We are not launching a crusade…but we are doing everything we can to protect the rights of the boys who are defendants in this case," Leibowitz said.[4]

The judge ruled to try the accused separately and Haywood Patterson was the only one brought to court. At the hearing, the first witness, John H. Green, Clerk of the Court of the Eight Judicial Circuit, said that he had seen more than 2500 jurors in Morgan County and "not one of them was a colored man."[5]

After Green stepped down, Leibowitz called Dr. Frank Sykes to take the stand. Appearing calm, he rose with a manner of self-confidence. Smartly dressed and standing almost six feet tall, the thirty-six-year old dentist was light-skinned, slender built and sported a mustache and a thick mane of nearly straight black hair. He earned a Bachelor's of Arts degree from Howard University, in Washington, DC, and then graduated from the university's School of Dentistry in 1918. Sykes came from a well-to-do family who were prominent civic leaders, politicians and business owners in town. The former Black Sox baseball player returned home in 1927 and opened a thriving dental practice.

Stepping into the witness box, Dr. Sykes sat down, crossed his legs, and pulled a paper from his breast pocket. He explained that the defense counsel asked him to prepare a list of "colored citizens," who were honest, intelligent and esteemed in the community. Sykes then began to read the names of 112 male citizens (omitting doctors) considered suitable for juror panels.

Knight rose to cross. "You don't know that the Jury

Commission just arbitrarily excluded those names, do you?" he asked in a condescending manner.

Responding politely but authoritatively, Sykes replied: "I don't know. I don't know how the Jury Commission selected the names...I don't know whether my color was considered or not."

A quick volley of words and objections between the attorneys went on for some while. Knight's curt sarcasm brought out roars of contemptuous laughter among courtroom spectators. Appalled at their reaction, Leibowitz jumped to his feet, waved his hands and shouted, "I am tired of some people making a Roman holiday out of this case."

The judge cautioned the court, "No laughter."

Knight indignantly scoffed, "I too am tired of Roman holidays so far as Alabama is concerned."[6]

Dr. Sykes maintained his composure, and once the courtroom quieted, he confidently said: "I am an educated man. I know what arbitrarily means...a man acts arbitrarily when he does things without regard to reason or justice."[7]

Next, the defense called Dr. Newlyn E. Cashin. The Cashin clan was also a well-known family in the community. Newlyn's father, Herschel V. Cashin, had been among the first black attorneys in town, and in 1892, President William McKinley appointed him receiver of monies at Huntsville. "...In all my life in Morgan County. I have never known of a single instance where any colored man of the African race was called to serve as a juror... in any part of the State," he admitted. A physician for twenty-four years, Cashin had attended Phillips Exeter Academy in New Hampshire. He later graduated from Howard University's Medical School (1908). Closely acquainted with individuals on Dr. Sykes' list, in addition to naming others, he stated that all were qualified but none never drawn as jurors.[10] When interrogated about Leo Sykes, a legally blind World War 1 veteran, Cashin sharply announced that his disability did not affect his mental reasoning.

Following him, a fifty-five year old plasterer took his seat in the witness box. He was dressed in a dark suit, white shirt, matching tie and kerchief. A descendant of early pioneers in town, Hulett J. (Hewlett or H. J.) Banks was the son of Matthew H. Banks, a well-respected former city alderman. Hulett had lived in Decatur all his life and was employed as a bill poster for over twenty-seven years. With pride he boasted that he had been voting for the last fifteen years.

The courtroom drama intensified when Leibowitz asked, "Did you have to pass certain tests to become a voter?" Objecting to the validity of voter eligibility, Knight strongly contended that one does not have to vote to be a juror. Patterson's attorney argued that voting demonstrated the ability to read and write. A melee of words erupted between the defense and prosecuting lawyers.

In Alabama, before African-Americans could exercise their right to vote under the 15th Amendment, they were required to recite and explain portions of the U.S.

---

[10] Dr. Cashin stated that he had full knowledge of the qualifications of individuals on Dr. Frank Sykes list and included others as well. Stanley Basham, J. H. Harris, William Gee, Abe Long, William Craig, William James, Phillip Lightfoot, I. Z. Moore, Charlie Montgomery, Will Terry, Rev. Womack, Rev. John Watkins, Rev. W. A. Wilhite, Rev. Newby, Rev. George Eldridge, Rev. U. G.[Ulysses[Draper, John Dilon, J. J. Jackson, Robert Jackson, E. Owens,

Constitution, as well as perform other aptitude skills required by the state to vote.[11]

Banks was poised and spoke in a calm and precise manner. "I come to court as a spectator every chance I get...I have never seen in my life any Negroes step up as jurymen." He then pulled a list that he had prepared from his pocket, and began to read the names of men believed to meet jury criteria. Under cross-examination, Attorney General Knight attempted to misconstrue and attack his statement, concerning the omission of black jurors. "I refuse to answer your question," said Banks.[8] The State Prosecutor was stunned, dazed, and shocked by his response. Livid, his face turned beet red and his hard, cold eyes flickered; as he attempted to regain control and shake off his anger.

After the wounding words, Knight badgered the witness again and again, about the character and standing of men on his list. "What is it you are holding back, tell us all about him (Ben Hayes)."

Leibowitz sharply interrupted, "Mr. Banks has not included Hayes in his list. It's immaterial."

Again, the courtroom cackled with laughter. Responding to another obnoxious outburst, Judge Horton testily rapped on his bench to ensure order. The court

---

[11] The 15th Amendment to the Constitution granted African American men the right to vote by declaring that the "right of citizens of the United States to vote shall not be denied or abridged by the United States or by any state on account of race, color, or previous condition of servitude." Although ratified on February 3, 1870, the promise of the 15th Amendment would not be fully realized for almost a century. Through the use of poll taxes, literacy tests and other means, Southern states were able to effectively disenfranchise African Americans. It would take the passage of the Voting Rights Act of 1965 before the majority of African Americans in the South were registered to vote.

warned that he would not tolerate any more snickering. When the room quieted, Banks unflinchingly answered back: "I don't know anything wrong with Ben Hayes." [9]

Admitting that he had known two of the jury commissioners for years, the witness further added: "I never saw any going around the colored sections of this county…to find any colored person qualified to serve on a jury."[10]

The Reverend Lester (L. R.) Womack was the next witness summoned to testify. He pastored First Baptist Church (African American Congregation) on Vine Street since 1931. The membership numbered about three hundred eighty. Rev. Womack acknowledged that he had never known any "colored persons" ever being examined for jury. He too, said that no one at any time notified him of their intentions to include the names of blacks on the rolls.[11] Pastor Womack also provided a list of names, specifying men he believed to be suitable for potential jurors.

Following him, James J (J.J.) Sykes, uncle of Dr. Frank Sykes, took the stand. He too, had been a lifetime resident of Decatur and was well respected by all. Born ten years after slavery was abolished, his white father (Frank Sykes) once owned his mother Laura, a mulatto, who had been a wedding present to Frank's wife. Laura bore the elder Sykes six children; J.J. was the youngest.

A sharp-witted intelligent businessman, J.J. Sykes owned a moving picture theatre on Vine Street. He also sold insurance, was part owner of a funeral home, and a notary public. In addition, he once operated a large coal yard, saloon and tailoring shop. He had been a member of the First Baptist Church for more than thirty years.

Under oath and with great pride, Sykes said that he had been voting since 1901. Ironically, the Alabama Constitution had been revised that same year to disenfranchise blacks. The amended version included separate public facilities, separate schools for "whites and colored," and denied countless blacks the right to vote with a literacy test and poll taxes. Often reinforced by acts of terror, these Jim Crow laws were designed to fuel segregation.

When Alabama's 1901 constitution banned burials of blacks and whites together, J.J. Sykes purchased land to provide a final resting place. White citizens complained. He boldly admitted that he was not violating the law and posed the question, "Negroes must bury their dead somewhere, what are they to do?" reported *The Decatur Daily.*[12]

Sykes further explained that he often discussed politics with citizens and neighbors, and said he believed in the Constitution of the United States. He likewise stated that he had never been asked to serve on a jury nor been examined by the Jury Commission. Presenting a list that bore the names of men he was personally acquainted with and perceived to be eligible for jury service, he revealed: "There are many more negroes besides these who possess the qualifications." One after another, Sykes looked at the

---

[12] Alabama's 1901 Constitution made it illegal for African Americans to be buried in white cemeteries. That same year, J.J. Sykes purchased property for a "Negro cemetery." The Magnolia-Sykes cemetery is the final resting place for former slaves, physicians, ministers, educators, business owners, farmers, and military veterans dating back to the Civil War, as well as, many of Decatur's early African American residents. The cemetery was the primary burial place for Blacks until 1965. The historic Magnolia-Sykes cemetery was listed on the Alabama Historic Cemetery Registry, August 2010.

names on the other lists, interjecting that some of the men had even served their country during World War I.

Under cross examination, he acknowledged to Attorney General Knight, "I served on a United States jury eight or nine years ago, but never on a jury in this county."[12]

By the time the Rev. William Jenkins Wilson took the stand, an even bitter veil of hostility infiltrated the courtroom walls. When Prosecuting Attorney Knight asked if he regarded men who had been sent to jail as "possessing qualities for jurors," Wilson said in a forceful and persuasive manner: "In Alabama, a colored man being sent to jail, did not always mean that he was a criminal. In all my life no man that I know of, black or white has ever said a single word against my reputation, honor or integrity."[13] Denouncing the allegation of being a communist, he proudly announced that he was a card-carrying member of the Republican Party, and "I do not belong to the Lily White or black and tan section of the party." He added that he took part in the affairs of his people and participated in political matters.

Born in Matthews, Alabama, Wilson was principal of the Gibbs Street (colored) school that later became known as Carver Elementary School. He also pastored St. Luke Baptist Church in Athens. Wilson earned degrees from both State Teachers College (presently Alabama State University) in Montgomery and Fisk University at Nashville.

Following him, Professor James (J.E.) Pickett testified on behalf of the defense. After reviewing the lists, he stated that he was "reasonably acquainted" with many of the men whose names had been presented. Continuing, the witness said that he knew what the words *moral turpitude* and *esteem* meant. He went on to state that, "I have never seen a negro on a jury nor do I know any of these negroes who names I have read as qualified on this list ever to have been summoned for jury duty. I have never been asked to perform jury duty."[14]

Professor Pickett attended Alabama A&M College (Alabama A&M University at Normal) earning a Bachelor's of Science degree in 1923. He was a member of the (Macedonia) Presbyterian Church on Cherry Street. Hired by the Decatur Board of Education, he had been serving as principal of the Decatur Negro High School for nearly 20 years. The school employed eight teachers and about 500 students attended.

Arguments continued in an effort to prove that blacks had been purposefully omitted from jury rolls. The next witness, Robert S. Bridgeforth, said that "he never knew of any one of them (Blacks) ever being called for jury duty in Morgan County...in the Circuit Court or County Courts."[15] Standing 5 feet 5 inches with a brown complexion, ebony hair and chestnut brown eyes, the former World War I veteran ran a pool hall on Vine Street. For thirty-seven years, he had lived on Second Avenue North (Cashin Street). After looking over all the lists, he testified that he knew most of the men on the Womack list and all those on Banks' list.

Next, George H. Reynolds, a local undertaker stepped into the witness box. Born in Hillsboro, Alabama, his father, Edward "Doctor" Reynolds was a well-known businessman who owned enormous tracts of land in Lawrence County. Reynolds moved to Decatur during the early twenties and attended Alabama A&M College at Normal, Morehouse College at Atlanta, Georgia, Fisk

University in Nashville, and the Washington College of Embalming in Chicago, Illinois. Viewing the lists, he too surmised that all were men of good integrity, and he believed to be fit to sit on a jury. Reynolds finished:

> I do not know whether or not I was ever considered as a qualified juror or whether or not the Jury Commission ever considered... any of the other names on these lists you have identified. All are good men, as far as I know.[16]

A forty-four year old dentist, Dr. Willis J. Wood, followed him. Wood graduated from both Tuskegee Institute and the Meharry Medical College at Nashville, where he received a dentistry degree. He was married and lived in the county for seventeen years. While testifying, he indicated that he had been a member of the First Baptist Church and was affiliated with the Negro Civic League, the Masons, (where he held the position of Master) and the Elks club (position of Exalted Ruler for colored people). He engaged in social events in the community and said that he had been a "good law-abiding citizen." Like his counterparts, he concluded, "I have never seen a colored man of African descent on a jury in Morgan County, nor heard of any."[17] After evaluating the four lists and ruling out the people he did not know, the dentist said the men were of good character and sound judgment. Under cross-questioning, Wood told Knight that he lived in a "white and colored" neighborhood. Despite that fact, he did not know whether the names of blacks were considered for jury boxes.

The last African American to be called to prove that there was a lack of inclusion of blacks on juries, was Dr.

Newman M. Sykes. Born in Decatur, he graduated from the "Negro" City School, Shaw University in Raleigh, North Carolina, and received a Bachelor of Science degree from Fisk College in Nashville, Tennessee. Additionally, he had earned a Medical degree from the University of Illinois, and worked nine years for the county. After returning home to Decatur, Sykes was the medical director for the Liberty Bell Insurance Company and often gave lectures on health to local churches and schools. He was also a member of the Masons, Pythians, and numerous civic organizations and fraternities.

Sykes testified that he had heard of blacks serving on juries prior to the 1901 disenfranchisement laws. He stated that he assisted in preparing the four lists, and knew others, whose names had not been included, but were well-qualified to serve on the juries. Questioning Alabama's jury process and the absence of blacks, Leibowitz asked, "Would you consider that a mere coincidence, or would you consider they have been kept from serving as jurors by reason of their race and color?" Knight objected.[18]

Arthur J. Tidwell, was the only witness called by the State to disprove the evidence. President of the jury board, he had been appointed to the office in 1931, by then Governor Benjamin Miller. His colleagues were J. Tomlinson and W. J. Briscoe. A venire of 100 names had been prepared in Morgan County for Haywood Patterson's trial. Sheriff Davis was summoned to produce the large crimson red book, marked *Jury Roll 1931* (names in the book had been kept secret and were from 1932 and 1933 registers).

"I am familiar with the duties of my office, with Section 14…which requires me to put on the jury roll all male citizens possessing the qualifications," answered Tidwell.[13] After reviewing several pages with more than 2000 plus names on the confidential jury roll, he finally admitted that while only the names of whites were listed, blacks were not omitted because of racial discrimination. He surmised that the Board had not known a Negro capable of serving based on the State statues. One man was overheard saying to another, "We've never had niggers in our juries yet and we never will...If we told them they could, there isn't a nigger here who would dare to try to sit on a jury," reported *The New York Times*.[19] Tidwell later justified the County's actions, saying that commissioners have discretionary powers even if blacks had been omitted from the rolls. Later, Commissioner Tidwell was given the four lists with the names of African American men. After reviewing the documents, he determined that some of the men had been considered.

"Were they excluded because of their color?" asked the State Prosecutor.

"No Sir," said Tidwell.

Later, under cross-examination, Tidwell underwent a lengthy interrogation. The vitriolic back and forth

---

[13] "The jury commission shall place on the jury roll and in the jury box the names of all male citizens of the county who are generally reputed to be honest and intelligent men, and are esteemed in the community for their integrity, good character and sound judgment, but no person must be selected who is under twenty-one or over sixty-five years of age, or, who is an habitual drunkard, or who, being afflicted with a permanent disease or physical weakness is unfit to discharge the duties of a juror, or who cannot read English, or who has ever been convicted of any offense involving moral turpitude. If a person cannot read English and has all the other qualifications prescribed herein and is a freeholder or householder, his name may be placed on the jury roll and in the jury box." See Gen. Acts, Alabama, 1931, No. 47, p. 59.

between the high-spirited lawyers resonated loudly, across the courtroom, whirling with "objections." At last, the judge's soft-spoken voice quieted the room, and the court recessed.

After reconvening, Leibowitz revealed that he was prepared to call every single black person on the list to appear in court. By this time, Judge Horton was fed up with the flood of witnesses; "motion denied," he hammered. Astonished at his ruling, the lead defense counsel asked if he understood correctly that sufficient evidence had been presented to establish (*prima facie*) that the defendant's Fourteenth Amendment rights had been violated. "Yes, the burden of proof is on the State to show that the Jury Commission complied with the statute in making up the jury roll," the judge said. "I am going to deny the motion of the defense, let's get on with the trial."[20]

Now that the motion was disposed of, the way was cleared to select a jury and for the trial to begin. The box containing the names of one hundred venire men was brought before the judge. Each of the potential jurors stood before him and swore to administer justice without prejudice.

Leibowitz solicited the help of T.C. Almon, who was employed solely to assist with striking the jury. Black citizens also offered the defense input into the jury selection. When the box had been shaken and names drawn, the defendant's legal team and prosecuting attorneys began blasting the potential jurors with tough questions. Twenty-five were found to be exempt because of their bigoted views, five were released because they were against capital punishment, and four dismissed when they said they could not convict a man based on circumstantial circumstances.[21]

Despite the defense's determination to prove blacks had been omitted from juries in Morgan County, not one black person's name was included on the jury roll. Thus, on March 31, an all-white jury composed of twelve men was selected: Eugene D. Bailey, foreman and draftsman; John J. Bryant, farmer from Falkville; Eddie Edwards, filling station operator in Decatur; William Grimes, bookkeeper from Decatur; Robert L. Landers, unemployed; James F. Steward, Sr., Hartselle, merchant; J. Foreman Wallace, a farmer from Danville; Irvin Craig, local barber; Cecil Crawford, a Joppa farmer; John Davis, bookkeeper in Decatur; Eugene Graves, Decatur, banker; and Robert Kitchens, a salesman.

Impaneled and settled in the jury box, all the men looked as if they were going to church, wearing suits in various shades of black, blue, brown, and gray with white shirts and ties. While waiting for court to convene, they occupied their time talking to one another. Those sitting on the front row leaned back with their feet propped up on the brass railings. Several of them comfortably rocked back and forward in the heavy, wooden swivel jury chairs, their hats perched in their laps. All waited to be sworn in. After a short time, they raised their right hand and affirmed the jurors' oath.

From that moment on, the jury was sequestered. When court recessed for the day, they spent the nights in an eight-room suite at the Lyons Hotel. On Sunday morning, April 2, the jurors attended St. John Episcopal Church, where juryman Graves, was the vestryman,[22] according to *The Decatur Daily*. In his sermon, Peter Dennis, Rector of the church, admonished congregants, "We must enlarge our vision, we must banish hatred and hypocrisy," reported *The New York Times*. Later, a fundamental error for the *"sake of justice"* was made when the bailiff, Edward R. Britnell, admitted that he allowed jurors to make unsupervised phone calls.

Defense Witness List Subpoenaed
Source: Morgan County Archives

Dr. Frank Sykes
Photo: Courtesy of Morgan County Archives

Hulett (H. J.) Banks
Photo: Courtesy of the Schaudies-Banks-Ragland Collection

George Reynolds
Photo: Courtesy of Christopher Cowan

Dr. Newlyn Cashin *(right)*
Photo: Courtesy of Sheryll Cashin

Dr. Willis Wood
(Dentist)
Photo: Courtesy of Rebecca Wood Holbert

CHAPTER 6

DRAMATIC TESTIMONIES

On Monday, April 3, 1933, the first Decatur trial got under way, *State vs Haywood Patterson*. People gathered from all around the region. Inside the Morgan County Courthouse, the courtroom quickly filled up. Dozens of spectators also stood in the hot, sweltering hallway, moving and shifting patiently in segregated lines. Cameras clicked. Tapping typewriters ruled the room until lawyers asked that they be silenced. Telegraph offices had been placed on standby, waiting for the invasion of reporters. As soon as both sides announced "ready," witnesses for the state were sworn in.

At the defense counsel table, Haywood Patterson sat surrounded by his lawyers and National Guardsmen. Scattered about the desk were piles of paper and books. The defendant's dark brown skin blended with his short plastered hair, which was parted slightly toward the middle. Standing five foot ten inches tall, he wore blue faded-out overalls, a light colored shirt and tie, and a bulky sweater that was stretched and slightly frayed from wear. He looked a bit unnerved as he clung to an old rusty horseshoe and rabbit's foot for a good luck charm.

Mrs. Jane Patterson, the defendant's mother, and Mrs. Ada Wright (the Wright brother's mother) were among those in court. During the trial, Mrs. Patterson stayed at a residence in the black quarters, across the street from the courthouse.[1] The tiny African American neighborhood contained mostly old and weathered but neat, double tenant and single-family clapboard dwellings. The shanties were a sharp contrast to the towering residences that existed in what is now known as Old Decatur Historic District.

An intense and edgy silence hovered over the courtroom when the State called its leading witness. Victoria Price (nicknamed Big Leg) wore a new stylish black dress with a white fichu near her neckline. A dark pillbox hat with a red feather covered her cropped hair, secured in place with bobby pins. The hat was paired with a matching purse. As she moved toward the witness box, her squeaky shoes whined with each step. Slowly climbing onto the platform and sitting down, she crossed her pale legs, revealing silk stockings. When the indictment was read, "not guilty" was Patterson's plea.

Questioning Price was State Solicitor Harle (H. G.) Bailey; he had been the Jackson County prosecutor during the first trials. The Georgia native was tall, slender and had gray eyes. After preliminary questions, Mrs. Price politely expanded and recapped the deplorable accounts of the so-called brutal attacks, just two years earlier.

In a voice loud enough to be heard all over the courtroom, Price conveyed how she and Ruby Bates boarded a freight train traveling from Chattanooga to Huntsville. Jumping onto an oil tanker first, they later moved to a gondola car carrying chert. A short time afterwards, seven white boys jumped into the car near Stevenson, five or ten minutes later, twelve "colored boys" also climbed into the car.

"Was this defendant among them?" Prosecutor Bailey asked.

"Yes Sir," admitted Victoria."[2]

"Now tell the court what happened," he said.

"Well, those niggers came jumping into the gondola and yelled, 'All you white sons of _____ unload.'"[3] According to Price, a fight broke out and all the white boys were thrown off the train except Orville Gilley.

"What became of him?" asked the prosecutor.

He crawled back in the gondola, she replied. "He said he was scared...and if us girls died, he would die too." Price further testified that she was wearing overalls, a shirt, three dresses, and a pair of step-ins, a girl's coat and girl's hat. "One of them – this nigger over there had a pistol," she said, pointing at Haywood Patterson "and another one had a knife...He pulled out his pistol and started shooting over the side of the gondola car."[4]

Without embarrassment and without batting an eye, Price proceeded with the sordid and graphic details. Animatedly, she told the court that one of the accused took a knife and held it to her throat, while another struck her on the head with the butt of his gun and blood trickled from her forehead. Six of the Negroes assaulted her and six attacked Ruby Bates as the train thundered toward Huntsville, she recalled. Her assailants pulled off her overalls and savagely ripped off her panties. Gripping her arms and legs, they pushed her down on to the sharp chert and held her while each of them took terms violating her. The last one finished only a few minutes before the train stopped at Paint Rock. She collapsed and couldn't remember anything until she woke up in a grocery store at Paint Rock, Victoria testified.[5]

In a sensational and obviously calculating move, Bailey, then pulled a pair of white torn cotton panties from his briefcase and asked, "Are those the step-ins you had on, on that occasion?"

Price replied, "Yes sir."

Had she washed them, asked the prosecutor?

"Yes sir," she responded.

At that point, the State offered the panties as new evidence. Flying to his feet Leibowitz shouted:

> We object to them, this is the first time in two years any such step-ins have ever been shown in any court of justice. They were not produced at the first trial or second trial or any of the four trials at Scottsboro. This is the first time in two years any step-ins have been produced in any court.[6]

About the same time, Knight vaulted out of his seat, screaming, "They are here now!" The entire room echoed with a thunderous roar of laughter. To everyone's surprise, Knight picked up the underpants, turned and flung them through the air, sending them sailing onto a jurors lap. Once more, the courtroom snickered loudly.[7]

Judge Horton slammed his wooden gavel nonstop. The room went silent. Horton cautioned, "The court has the right to clear the courtroom...If you cannot restrain your feelings in this courtroom, the proper place for you is on the outside."[8]

Yielding, Leibowitz withdrew his objection exclaiming, "Let the exhibit go into evidence."[9] The panties were entered by the State.

Questioning resumed. "Now, tell the court what happened." Bailey urged. Uninhibited and step by step, without reservation, Ms. Price picked up the conversation where she left off, providing explicit details of the so-called attack. By the time she finished her squalid story, several women in court held their heads shamefully down with humiliation. As the state finished their interrogation, the accuser stared at Haywood Patterson, then raised her hand and once again pointed her finger at him, accusing the defendant of attacking her. After a total of sixteen minutes, she ended her inflammatory testimony for the State. The witness was then turned over to the defense.

Samuel Leibowitz stood and walked toward the supposed victim. He asked gently, "Miss Price, shall I call you Miss Price or Mrs. Price?"

"Mrs. Price," she insisted in a clear and sharp voice.[10] Price was her maiden name and at the time she was still married to Enos McClendon, her second husband. The two worked together in the cotton mill and had been separated because of a shooting incident.

Price's testimony was interrupted when the chief defense attorney asked Robert S. Turner, of Sheffield, Alabama (conductor on the train), to assist him with assembling a colorful 32-foot miniature train. Termed the "Scottsboro Special," the small-scaled train set was put together on a table directly in front of the jury box.[11] It was an exact replica of the southern freight that the two women said the brutal attack occurred on.

Recalling Victoria Price to the stand, the defense counsel began a masterful argument on the whereabouts of all those riding the train. Stubbornly, however, his witness would not admit the train's similarities. To the question of whether or not the model was a fair representation and what the differences were, she remarked: "… Them are toys, and don't look like the train we rode."[12] Later she brazenly declared, "I can't explain – I won't explain."[13]

In an attempt to poke holes in her previous testimony and show inaccuracies, Leibowitz first pressed her on the details of the claimed rape. He then took jabs at flaws in her unscrupulous character and attempted to introduce arrest reports and convictions for prostitution, vagrancy and adultery. The prosecutor and defense lawyers clashed repeatedly.

During the defense's interrogation, the lead attorney revealed that Ms. Price had not only been married twice, but that she also had a boyfriend, Leroy "Jack" Tiller, who was a married man with children. He then suggested that the relationship with Price led to Tiller's divorce. Leibowitz also conveyed that both Tiller and his wife had worked at the cotton mills with Price. Intending to prove that she was a prostitute, the attorney for the defendant presented a copy of a recent indictment in Huntsville.[14]

"Objection!" the chief prosecutor commanded. Ruling the evidence inadmissible, the judge determined that the adultery charges had nothing to do with Ms. Price's credibility.

Pivoting for a moment with his cross-examination, Leibowitz insisted that Victoria Price had spent time at Kate Lackner's. "Miss Kate" was a well-known madam, who ran a "gentlemen's sporting house" in Decatur at the end of Bank Street. Denying the claim and seething with anger, Price displayed very little patience with this line of questioning. Her hard face and piercing, dark eyes brandished utter abhorrence. "You can't prove that," she roared.[15]

Price had lied about her age when she was arrested. Leibowitz asked how she could have been twenty-one two years ago, and twenty-seven now?

Mrs. Price sassed: "I ain't that educated to figure it out."[16]

Interrogating her about resistance to her attackers, the defense asked, "Did you bite, kick, or scratch?"

She answered, "I don't know, I won't say. I just fought."[17] Each time there was a contradiction of her testimony, she would conveniently suffer from memory lapses. Often the handy amnesia was combined with taunting responses, such as "I've answered that four times," or she would spurt "You can't prove that."[18] Frequently, she annoyingly blurted, "That's some of Ruby's dope (dope is slang for shady story)," reported *The Decatur Daily*.[19] Every so often in an attempt to evade a question, she would snap, "You talk to (*sic*) fast" or "It's been two years and I don't recollect."

"Did you fight?" "Were you tired?" "Why was the white boy allowed to stay on the train to witness the crime committed on two white women?" "Why wasn't your coat submitted as evidence since it had male gametes on it?" Subjected to long and rigorous questioning, the state's witness was pressed by the defense attorney to relate the details. Every now and then Mrs. Price's temper flared, her face turned red, and her body shook with anger, as she clenched her jaw tightly. During the cross-examination, an intense war of words escalated between Patterson's lawyer and the prosecutor. Finally, Judge Horton admonished the men to address the court rather than each other. During the long hours of questioning, Mrs. Price's eyes incessantly zipped back and forth to the prosecutor's table, eyeing him to make objections to the repulsive questioning. Her answers fired back at Samuel Leibowitz, with unwavering arrogance, brazenness and belligerence. A further attempt was made to show Price's loose character and to discredit her previous testimony, as Leibowitz probed her about Lester Carter.

> *Question:* "Mrs. Price, I am going to put a question to you, so please listen to it; I put it in all fairness and courtesy, I don't mean to be rude in any way. Did you know Lester Carter before this day, yes or no."
> *Answer:* "I never did know him."
> *Question:* "Didn't you leave with Lester Carter?"
> *Answer:* "Lester Carter wasn't with us on the train."

Fuming at the questioning, her face heated up like hot coals as she fidgeted in her chair. Unrelenting, Leibowitz swooped down on the alleged victim like a vulture at its prey. He drilled her about her intimacies with Jack Tiller, while with Bates and Carter in a Huntsville hobo jungle, just two nights before leaving for Chattanooga.[14] Enraged and not willing to back down, Price denied even knowing Carter. She testified that her first time meeting him was the day they were dragged off the train and taken to a Scottsboro jail.

Once more, Leibowitz attempted to expose Victoria's

---

[14] Hobo Jungle was a commune in certain areas of a town at or near railroad junctions, where vagrants would congregate waiting to jump a ride on an outgoing train. In the jungle, drifters would drink whiskey, cook (making campfires), eat, sleep, play cards and participate in a variety of other acts.

conviction for lewdness with Jack Tiller, which the witness emphatically denied. "We object," Knight said, arguing that the conviction was irrelevant. The court sustained the objection. "We don't care if this woman has been convicted of forty offenses...she has never been convicted for living in adultery with a negro," said the attorney general.[20]

"Did you tell the man by the name Lester Carter, you would find him a girl, then did you get Ruby Bates and introduce her to him?" Leibowitz asked.

Answering sharply, Price said: "No sir."

"Isn't it a fact that three days after you met Lester Carter, you and he, Tiller and Ruby Bates went walking along the L&N Railroad tracks?"

"No Sir, we never have been on the railroad together."

"Did you have intercourse with Tiller a short time before you left Huntsville?"

"No Sir. I have told you three times, and I am not telling you any more – no sir I didn't."[21]

Victoria explained that she and her friend Ruby Bates left Huntsville looking for work. Late that night, after arriving in Chattanooga, the women stayed at a boarding house run by a woman named Mrs. Callie Brochie. The rooming house was near the train depot, Price said. Making light of her statement Leibowitz asked, "By the way, Mrs. Price, ...the name of Mrs. Callie, is the name of a boarding house lady used in the *Saturday Evening Post* stories—isn't that where you got the name?"[22] (Sis. Callie Fluker was a fictional character, who ran a boarding house in a column that stereotyped blacks during the Jim Crow era.) Later investigations by the defense proved that no such person by that name lived in Chattanooga.

Knight objected. Price was furious, her face flushed as she squirmed in her chair.

Unmasking her carnal escapades, Leibowitz asked her sternly, "Didn't you and Gilley and Lester Carter and Ruby Bates go over a trestle near the railroad yards in Chattanooga and down a valley to where there was a clump of trees?"

"No sir," she fumed.

"Isn't it a fact you all want (went) over in the jungle (hobo jungle) there and built a fire?" he demanded.

"I didn't go to any jungles," she quaked.

Mrs. Price looked at him coldly. Disgusted with the chief defense attorney's insulting interrogations, her answers were harsh. She responded contemptuously to his insinuations that she fraternized with blacks.

> *Question:* "Do you know a negro by the name of Lewis that lives in a shack right near those railroad yards?"
> *Answer:* "I don't know any negroes, I am not associating with negroes."
> *Question:* "Isn't it a fact you had been to Lewis' house on many many occasions and several other occasions on prior trips?"
> *Answer:* "I never was in Chattanooga but one time in my life and that is when I went there searching for work the 24th day of March—I never was at any negro's house in my life."[23]

This was a hit on her character, because the Jim Crow South considered it to be inappropriate for any white woman to associate with or even converse with a black man.

Disrupting the questioning, a man in one of the rows

suddenly stood and yelled, "Let's get Leibowitz."[24] Two guards quickly removed the instigator out of the court and then searched him for weapons.

Reacting to her grand performance, the chief defense counsel said mockingly, "You are somewhat of an actress, are you not, Mrs. Price?"

"You're a pretty good actor yourself," she smirked.

A transcript of the trial held in Scottsboro was introduced by Patterson's attorney, with no objection from the state. The transcript was entered as evidence.

Interrupting Price's testimony, Leibowitz asked permission to call the train conductor, R. S. Turner. Identifying various cars on the "Scottsboro Special," he then said that when the train stopped at Paint Rock, a pistol and a Bruton snuff box was found in a gondola car. Under cross-examination, the chief prosecutor asked Turner if he knew the man who found the gun. "It was flagman Reese Allen," he stated. [25] Recalled to the stand under redirect and direct, Ms. Price continued with her account of the day of the alleged attack. After nearly three hours the grueling interrogation ended and the witness stepped down.

Dr. Robert R. Bridges, one of the Scottsboro doctors who examined Price and Bates an hour or so after the claimed assault, came forward as State's witness. The doctor recounted what he had previously said during the first trials. Under cross-examination, the defendant's attorney used the doctor's testimony to their advantage. In other trials, Victoria said that she had been bleeding and received bruises from the six who had allegedly gang raped her. According to Dr. Bridges, there was very little trauma, despite the women's supposedly violent ordeal.

He testified that Price had only a few scratches on the back part of her wrist and three or four blue spots on her back, about the size of a pecan. He and Dr. Marvin Lynch, the other examining doctor found no living spermatozoa from either of the women (live spermatozoa was expected to last around twelve hours). Dr. Bridges determined that no intercourse had recently occurred and that the women seemed unaffected with the day's traumatic events.[26]

Hearing this, the judge who had studied medicine leaned forward and probed Dr. Bridges about the alleged victims' emotional condition. "Did you observe the respiration at the time, whether they were breathing fast or slow—excitement?"

They were "practically normal," the doctor responded.

Judge Horton continued: "Did you notice their pulse and respiration the next morning?"

"Yes sir, they were crying, nervous and hysterical."[27] Dr. Bridges answered that only after spending the night in jail did the two women demonstrate any anxiety.

Another witness, Lee Adams, affirmed that he had seen two groups throwing punches in a car as the train passed his farm.[28] As Adams stepped down from the witness chair, the State produced its only eyewitness to the so-called attack, Ory (Ora) Dobbins, a farmer from Stevenson. Tall and slender, he sported a thick, faded soup bowl haircut. Sitting straight in the witness box, he crossed his legs displaying dark brogan work shoes. He wore typical farmers' clothes, bib overalls with straps that buckled over each shoulder, the unbuttoned side flaps opened to show the layer of light colored long sleeve shirts underneath the overalls.

"Where were they, what part of the train were they,

what sort of a car were they in?" started the prosecutor. Under direct examination, Dobbins admitted that he had seen some Negroes and a white woman near the back of the train. "I saw one of the girls setting *(sic)* up on the end of the gon (gondola) fixing to jump off." Leibowitz objected to the statement, "fixing to jump off." Motion overruled. Picking up where he left off Dobbins told the court, "I saw a negro grab her and throw her down just as the train passed into the cut."[29]

Prepared with official transcripts of previous trials before Judge Hawkins, the chief defense attorney maliciously tore into the deponent. He first presented photos of Dobbins house and barn as evidence to show where the train was passing, in conjunction with where he had been standing. Pointing to his exact location, the eyewitness explained that he was on his way to the barn to get his mule as the train went by. Dobbins testified that he was about forty feet from the tracks. Scoring a knockout punch, the defense litigator directed their attention to the model train set. Leibowitz then pointed out the maximum distances from halfway between the grindstone where Ory was seated; in comparison to the barn, as to where Attorney General Knight sat, then to the judge's bench (the railroad tracks). Unquestionably, the photographs demonstrated that it was impossible for Dobbins to have seen any action on the passing train. The barn would have blocked his view, disproving his previous testimony.[30]

To further discredit Dobbin's statement, Leibowitz grilled him on whether he saw one woman or two on the train. Reading from the transcript two years ago at Scottsboro, Dobbins acknowledged that he had seen two women. Judge Horton leaned forward in his chair, interrupting the questioning, "Did you state that you saw two girls, Yes or No?"

Evading the question, Dobbins wouldn't say for certain and later claimed he didn't remember. For the purpose of clearing up this discrepancy in the testimony, the judge searchingly asked, "She had on women's clothes?"[31]

Rattling the eyewitness, Leibowitz repeated the same question that Horton had asked. Dobbins pronounced: "She had on women's clothes."

Patterson's attorney asked, "What kind of clothes, overalls?"

"No sir, dress," the witness insisted.[32]

Expanding his account, Dobbins described one of the women as wearing a "brown coat."[33] This was a troubling response for the prosecutor's team. For two years, the fact that the two women had been disguised as men and were wearing men's caps, coats, and overalls, was widely talked about. Would his response spur a "not guilty" verdict?

Arthur Woodall, the fifth State witness, was medium built with blue eyes and brown hair. A second-generation dry-goods merchant in Stevenson, he was also a part-time sheriff deputy. Under oath, he testified that the seven white boys appeared at his store complaining that they had been thrown off the train. "One had his head cut open…and bloody all over, and another pretty bloody… the others were scratched up and bruised," he stated.[34]

Woodall, together with the sheriff and the accusers, left Stevenson to meet the posse at Scottsboro. The deputy explained that while searching the black men, he removed two knives (one with a long blade and the one Victoria Price had said her so-called attackers took off her) and a fifty cent piece. Earlier, he stated that Chief Deputy

Charles Simmons had seized one of the two knives from one of the blacks.[35]

Under cross-examination, the defense attorney probed Woodall intensely about the knives. "Did you ask the negro if it was his knife?"

"He said he took it off the white girl," the witness answered back.

Once again, counsel asked, "Did you ask him if it was his knife?"

The sheriff's deputy quickly remarked that he had himself confiscated it from "the white girl, Victoria Price."[36] The lead defense counsel was taken aback. At the first trial in Scottsboro, Woodall conveyed that he "searched all of these darkies" and took the knife from Clarence Norris.

Amused at Woodall's answers to the defense, in an outburst, the Attorney General laughed, slammed his hands on top of the table, jumped up and sprinted toward a nearby exit, and out of the courtroom. Offended, Leibowitz moved for a mistrial, recalling that he had not seen such deplorable action in his entire fifteen year career. In an effort to defuse the situation, Judge Horton announced that the chief prosecuting attorney regretted his action. When Knight returned to the courtroom, he concurred and apologized to the judge, jury and opposing counsel. "I did strike my hands, your honor and I am sorry. I ask that the jury disregard my action," quoted *The Decatur Daily*.

Urging the jury to disregard the prosecutor's inappropriate behavior, Judge Horton declared: "Gentlemen of the jury, don't consider that at all, that is not proper for you to consider, and do not let it influence you whatever."

Nonetheless, the motion for mistrial was overruled.[37]

The knife and fifty cents were taken from Price, Woodall said, contradicting the fact that Victoria said she didn't have any money.

On Wednesday, after the lunch recess was called, William A. Christal, a black man from Birmingham, Alabama, was brought to court. He testified that shortly before midnight, three white New Yorkers – Muriel Rukeyser (who would become a poet and political activist), Edward Sagarin, and Hank Fuller – as well as James Cooper, who was black, had been stopped in the "Negro section of town." The four of them were taken into custody and interrogated. When police checked out the address, where they said they were staying, they found Christal in the room. (In many instances, whites were intimidated via the criminal justice system for aiding blacks in the South.). The authorities confiscated publications from the National Student League and letters pertaining to the Scottsboro Trials.[38] Christal told Horton that the pamphlets were to raise money for the defense legal fund. The judge let him go free.

When court reconvened, the State continued to argue its case by calling William H. Hill, the Southern Railroad agent at Paint Rock. According to Hill, when the train stopped, he had seen some of the blacks jump off, while others remained in various cars. The women were off the train when he saw them. "They appeared excited and one of them was crying. One of them complained about being attacked," he said. Under cross-examination, Leibowitz asked, "You didn't expect to find any women on the train?"

"Yes sir," Hill echoed. The message had been transmitted by the operator, who had called ahead and stated that there were women on the train as well as "eight or ten negroes." Refusing to say that the women were hysterical, he explained that after hearing that the women had been attacked, he pointed to a shade tree near the tracks and told them to sit under it.

Tom Rossenau and Lee Adams appeared next as State witnesses. The prosecution rested.

CHAPTER 7

Damaging Confession

Aiming to destroy Victoria Price's credibility, the defense opened with a parade of witnesses. The first was Dallas Ramsey, a black man who lived in a small house adjacent to the Hobo Jungle in Chattanooga. When he had taken the stand, the chief defense counsel asked, "Did you see some girls that morning in the place called the jungle...some white girls?"

"Yes sir," the witness replied.

All of a sudden, Leibowitz called out, "Will you bring Victoria Price in?"[1]

Protesting, State Attorney General Knight barked, "We object to bringing her in until he describes her." Before Ramsey could answer any more questions, the judge interrupted, and asked what time he had seen the two women. Once again, the prosecutor objected loudly. Horton overruled saying, "Let her come in."

Identifying Price as the woman who approached him, Ramsey testified that she asked what time the train left for Huntsville. "Somewhere around nine," he answered. "We came up here hunting a job," Price told him.[2] Unable to find work, they were returning to Huntsville.

"Did you ask her how she was getting back to Huntsville?" Leibowitz asked. "Yes sir, she said she was going to hobo back." Ramsey had cautioned her, "It (hoboing) is a pretty hard way for a woman to travel."[3] He recalled seeing the two women, a little while later with a white man. The three of them were gathered over near the water tank where hoboes waited to hop the train.

Throughout the defense's questioning, prosecutor Knight repeatedly interrupted with objections.

"When the train run I seen (*sic*) them all catch the train there," Ramsey continued. Seeking clarification, the judge butted in and asked, "How many were there?" Ramsey answered, "I only seen two girls. I seen a crowd of boys, white and colored."[4]

Under cross, Knight suggested that Chamlee, one of the criminal defense attorneys, visited Ramsey about the case. The witness affirmed that Chamlee had spoken to him and Earnest (E. L.) Lewis, his next door neighbor. With reference to his first knowledge of the alleged assault, the prosecutor asked Ramsey for a second time.

> *Question:* "You are sure you read about it the next morning?"
> *Answer:* "Yes sir."
> *Question:* "What paper did you read it in?"
> *Answer:* "*Chattanooga Times.*"
> *Question:* "Did you tell anybody you had seen these girls?"
> *Answer:* "Yes Sir, told everybody around there I had seen them and had talked with them over there."

After that, Morris Payne testified. Later, the defense called Beatrice Maddox, a round-faced woman with smooth brown skin, wide eyes, and thick lips. She was the sister of Andy and Roy Wright and a long-time resident of Chattanooga. Under direct examination, she insisted that she had not been able to locate any person by the name of Callie Brochie who ran a boarding house or lived in Chattanooga for that matter. Nor was there anyone by that name in the telephone book. The defense entered the *Chattanooga City Directory* as evidence, casting doubt that such a person existed.

Under cross-examination, Knight mockingly queried Mrs. Maddox about her statements regarding the whereabouts of Callie Brochie and the directory that had been submitted. He first asked if she was "connected with the City of Chattanooga." When she responded, "I work," the prosecutor sarcastically questioned her about employment with the city of Chattanooga. She explained that she was "hired" in the city.

"You are not the mayor? You are not the alderman – you are not hired to compile the directory of people who live in Chattanooga?" hammered the attorney general.

"No," she answered patiently, unperturbed by his insistence.

Pounding, Knight charged, "You looked for Callie Brochie's name...Callie Brochie's address?"

She answered simply, "Yes, sir."

"Who asked you to look for it?"

"I take it own (*sic*) my own self to look at it," bragged Ms. Maddox.[5]

After Maddox's court appearance, several white men taunted Beatrice and her friends while they shopped at a local business in Decatur. "There is some of those witnesses for the Scottsboro boys, and they ought to be run out of town or killed."[6] Terrified and fearing for their lives, the women rushed out of the store.

George Chamlee, one of the defense attorneys, was the next to be sworn in and examined. For more than twenty-five years, he had lived or had a law office on Seventh Street in Chattanooga and knew many of the people who resided there. When asked if he was acquainted with anyone by the name of Callie Brochie, who lived and ran a boarding house in Chattanooga, he responded:

> No sir, I have examined the city directories for the years 1930, 1931 and 1932 to see if I could find any such name as Callie Brochie in Chattanooga, and I went from one end of Seventh Street to the other, and I have been over Seventh Street on an average of once or twice and sometimes ten times a day for forty years, and I don't believe there ever was a boarding house in Chattanooga owned by a woman named Callie Brochie, or such a woman has been in Chattanooga within the last three years.[7]

Following his testimony, Chamlee stepped down from the witness chair and returned to the defense table.

Violence was anticipated. The local newspaper reported that the two hardware stores sold out of ammunition while refusing to sell to blacks. Numerous reports of lynching mobs and Ku Klux Klan cross burnings were widespread. An underground network was formed to provide for the safety of the black reporters, moving them from house to house in the community. When Ted Poston was in Decatur covering the trial, he sat among the black spectators, dressed in old ragged clothes, and wrote his notes under his coat. He would later hand the notes to a New York reporter to wire his stories. On occasion, he would sneak to the depot and slip notes in the mail car. One time, some whites' caught him at Union Station and accused him of being a reporter. With fake preacher credentials, he passed as a minister.

According to the book, *Ted Poston: Pioneer American Journalist*, Poston was hired by *The New York Post* and became the first African-American staff reporter at an established newspaper. He later became editor of Harlem's *Amsterdam News* (a black paper) and reported on the Scottsboro Boys trials. Poston covered numerous stories about the heinous murders of blacks in the South, and events during the Civil Rights movement.

That Wednesday morning, Captain Burleson informed Judge Horton that a group of about two hundred men had convened in a lodge hall near the courthouse. Sheriff Davis admonished the group to withdraw. Davis later confirmed that rumors were circulating, but told the judge, "So far as I can ascertain, there is no truth to the reports." The group assembled only to express their outrage and dismay over Leibowitz's interrogation of the witnesses, he said.[8]

An edgy quiet crept over the room when Judge Horton briefly dismissed the jurors. His clear but sharp voice broke the silence as he announced, "If those defendants are guilty they should be punished. If they are not guilty, they should be acquitted. That is for the court and jury to establish." With booming authority he said, "Mob violence will not be tolerated." The words hung heavily in mid-air as he chided the spectators with piercing eyes. Horton continued with a firm warning that the guardsmen had orders "to shoot to kill."[9]

Forbidding any actions of violence or lynchings, the magistrate raised his typically quiet voice to a slightly higher pitch. Determined to protect the prisoners, their counsel, and anyone involved with the case, he assured the observers: "You've got to kill these guards before you'll get the prisoners." Defying any lynch mobs, he further announced that anyone who caused the death of any of the prisoners was "not only a murderer, but a cowardly murderer." Finally he declared, "I have spoken harsh words, but every word I say is true, and I hope we will have no more of any such conduct." The jurors returned to the courtroom.

Willie Roberson was the first of the defendants put on the stand to testify in Patterson's trial. Under direct examination he told the court that he boarded a tank car and remained there until the train stopped at Stevenson. Then he got into a box car. He was on his way to Memphis to get medical treatment. Suffering from syphilis and gonorrhea for about nine months, he was in excruciating pain. The oozing lesions made it difficult for him to walk, and he used a cane to ambulate. Roberson said that the doctor at Scottsboro examined him after he was arrested, and observed the large "shankers" (chancres) on his body.

While questioning the witness, Leibowitz asked, did you "jump off of a box car into a gondola car and engaged in a fight...wrestling...and scuffling...and engaged in raping her (Victoria Price) or the other girl?"

In a loud and roaring voice, prosecutor Knight screamed, "We object!"

"Let me finish," said Leibowitz.[10]

Judge Horton sustained the objection.

Upon resuming his testimony, Roberson insisted he had not raped any one. He had not seen any women on the train, nor had he seen a fight. When the witness was ordered off the train, a white man was also riding in the car with him. "We just want the negroes off," a deputy told them. After being removed from the train, all the blacks were taken to a nearby store, tied with a rope and hauled onto the bed of a truck. When they reached the Scottsboro jail, Roberson recalled: "One of the fellows talked about taking us out there and hanging us to a tree with a rope."[11]

Attorney General Knight interrogated Roberson about his reasons for leaving Atlanta and going to Tennessee for medical treatment as well as how long he'd stayed in Chattanooga. The witness said that he spent one night in Chattanooga, and that he had been allowed to stay at the police station in the City Hall. "No," he had not been arrested, he added.[12]

Attempting to prove that he was lying, the cross-examining attorney grilled him at length about knowing Ozie Powell. Roberson maintained that he was not acquainted with Powell until Scottsboro.

Olen Montgomery was the next witness called. Nearly totally blind, he told the court that he jumped on an oil tanker as the train rolled out of Chattanooga. He was alone until the train reached Paint Rock. Like Roberson, he testified that he was going to Memphis, seeking medical treatment and that he had neither seen any women during the trip nor did he rape anyone. Throughout the cross examination, the skilled prosecutor aggressively interrogated the witness.

After him, Ozie Powell was called and sworn in. He too stated that he had not participated in the fight and like the others had not seen any white women on the train. During the cross-examination by Knight, Leibowitz objected frequently.

The next person to come forward for the defense was Andy Wright. He explained that his younger brother, Roy, and friends Eugene Williams and Haywood Patterson got on the train at East 23rd Street. It was a distance of a mile or less from all of their homes. Wright said trouble started around the time they were passing through the Lookout Mountain tunnel. The white guys intentionally stepped on their hands. Confronting the white men, Patterson told them to let him know the next time they wanted to get by and he would move. An argument followed. Rocks were thrown.

Other blacks came into the car and complained about the white boys also harassing them. A fight broke out. One of the blacks pulled out a pistol and hit one of the white men in the head. All but two of the white males jumped off the train, he said. The man with the pistol attempted to force one of them off as well, but Haywood Patterson saved him. The man with the gun jumped off the train soon after the fight.[13]

Roy Wright once stated that he had been coerced into accusing his co-defendants of attacking the women in previous trials. During a March 1933 interview, the younger Wright told how they were beaten and threatened if they did not admit to what the authorities told them to say. On the day of the arrest at Scottsboro, one of the guards stabbed him with a bayonet in his right cheek. Wright stated that the women were brought into the jail on two previous occasions, but, they did not recognize them. When they were brought in the third time, he said, the women accused them as their attackers.

Following Andy Wright's testimony, Eugene Williams was called to take the stand. He affirmed that he had been on death row at Kilby Prison for two years, even though the U.S. Supreme Court reversed the death sentence. Williams's story coincided with that of Andy Wright. In his soft-spoken voice, he told how the white men threw rocks at them. Afterwards, some of the whites had words with Patterson about stepping on his hand. One of the men said, "What do you care if I knock you off? It will be one negro out of the way." A fight ensued. Later when asked if he saw any women on the train, "I didn't see 'nairn," Williams responded.[14] Under questioning by the state prosecutor, he divulged that he kept a small knife but never took it out of his pocket. The witness denied seeing any women until they got to Paint Rock.

Taking the stand next was defendant Haywood Patterson. Recounting the fight, his story was similar to that of the other defendants. Giving specifics about his daring deed to save one of the white men, he said "The train was going to (*sic*) fast. I was afraid the boy would get killed." Just as the train picked up speed, Gilley (who had been involved in the fight) scurried down the ladder on the side of a tank car. Hanging dangerously and swaying from the side of the fast-moving locomotive, a black hand moved to push him backward. Fearing Gilley would be killed, Patterson intervened: "I pulled this white boy back up on the train and saved his life."[15] Andy Wright, one of the accused, helped him. The man with the pistol and others had gotten off the train after the fight, he added.

Patterson also disclosed that the brown pants he wore the day of the alleged attack, were examined by authorities when he got to the Scottsboro jail. Nothing incriminating showed on them and the trousers had not been confiscated.

Examination by the state prosecutor was vicious. The attorney general growled a barrage of questions. He asked the defendant if he mocked how the girl cried during the attack while he was at Kilby Prison. Time and again, Patterson rejected the accusation, he staunchly, denied seeing any girls on the train. Often, Knight referenced questions from the official trial transcript at Scottsboro. "You were tried at Scottsboro?" the prosecutor queried.

"Yes sir, I was framed in Scottsboro," Haywood replied.

"Who told you to say that?" demanded Knight.

"I told myself to say it," responded Patterson.

Leibowitz broke in, "I have treated your witnesses with the utmost courtesy." With a gesture, he indicated that he had not shouted, pointed his finger or tried to embarrass any of them.

"I am not ashamed of how I am examining this witness," shouted Knight.[16] Under re-cross and re-direct, the attorneys continued to reel sharp jabs back and forth. When there were no further questions, the witness stepped down.

A fireman on the train, Percy Ricks, was called by the defense. As Chamlee examined him, he gave details about the train's speed, rail slopes, and other facts about its operation. Describing the arrest of the black youth at Paint Rock, he said that an army of men with guns was waiting at the depot. He had seen the two women and a white man earlier, when the train stopped at Stevenson. Under cross-examination, Mr. Ricks informed the Morgan County Solicitor, Wade Wright, that when the train stopped at Paint Rock, the women got off and started running in one direction. After seeing the posse, they turned and ran another way.

Dr. Edward A. Reisman, an expert witness for the defense, was next. A physician at Erlanger Hospital in Chattanooga, the doctor presented charts that gave a precise anatomical description of the female organs. After a detailed and extensive explanation of the human body, he concluded that a woman going through such an ordeal would have an increased "pulse or respiration."

Following Reisman, Lester Carter, another defense witness was called to take the stand. His blond hair was well-groomed and his slim face clean shaven. Well-dressed, he wore a double-breasted tweed suit and dark polished shoes. Even though he went with the women to Chattanooga and was taken off the train with the alleged victims at Paint Rock, this was the first time he had been summoned to testify.

Speaking in a fast, high-pitched voice Carter revealed that he had been serving time in a Huntsville jail for hoboing (vagrancy) in 1931. That is when he met Jack Tiller. Around the same time, he became acquainted with the two women. Victoria Price had been an inmate in the jail, and Ruby Bates had come to visit her. When Carter and Tiller were released, the men went to the mill to let the women know that they were out of jail.[17]

The next evening, the foursome met and went into the woods near the Huntsville railroad yards. Leibowitz asked Carter if he had seen Victoria Price and Jack Tiller being intimate. He answered, "Yes," and stated that when it started raining, the couples found an empty box car and remained there until early the next morning.

We talked and started planning this hobo trip; they
said they wanted to go to Chattanooga, or some town
away from there. That they were getting sick of the
place at the mill, it didn't pay enough wages, and
we could go some place, and they could "hustle" the
town and Jack and I could get a job and work and
have that much money between us four.[18]

Later that day, Carter, Price, and Bates hopped the
train, at a point near the "Negro cemetery" in Huntsville.
Tiller went along with them to their "jump-on point," but
didn't leave with them. His plan was to join them once
they got settled.

When the threesome arrived in Chattanooga, they
had no money. "We were walking around and looking
for some place to sleep," Carter said. A little while later
Orville Gilley, also known as "Carolina Slim," joined
them. He was tall and slim and said he was familiar with
the hobo jungle. Around eight that evening, the four of
them located a spot, built a fire, and spent the night there.
Carter's account differed from that of Victoria Price, who
said she spent the night at Callie Brochie's house. Early
the next morning, the men had gone over to Rossville
Boulevard to "bum breakfast." When they returned, the
women had moved to a different area in the hobo jungle
and were sitting by a campfire in the midst of several
black men. After rejoining their hobo companions, the
women accused the blacks of using bad language in their
presence. At their urging, they insisted that Carter go
over and whip them. "I had a small pearl handle knife,"
the witness said.

The prosecutor and defense attorneys got into a verbal
sparring match. Occasionally, spectators snickered or

laughed out loud. Judge Horton rapped his gavel to bring order in the court.

Continuing, the witness repeated a conversation he overheard after being detained by the Jackson county authorities. "Play like you are my brother," Victoria told Odel Gladwell, one of the men involved in the fight. "If you don't, we will be arrested for hoboing." "It is ok with me, I will be your brother," Gladwell said.[19] Then, with a bit of anger, Victoria threatened Carter and said if he did not agree to her story, she'd see to it that he didn't testify.

Fast and furious, Wade Wright, the prosecuting attorney, hit with hard and intense punches. To question Carter's character the prosecutor brought up a past conviction, "You stole this man's clothes," revealing why Carter had been in the Huntsville jail.

"I object," screamed Leibowitz.[20] The judge overruled.

Carter offered more details about the women during the short time that they were in the Chattanooga jungle. "They were sitting there close by the Negroes, you know, touching distance, rubbing against one another."[21] While on the way back to Huntsville, some white boys approached him about forcing the blacks off the train. "They said they didn't want the Negroes riding on the same train they were," Carter recalled.[22] When the freight slowed down near Stevenson, the annoyed white men climbed off the train, picked up rocks and began to throw them at the blacks. Gladwell and Ferguson started the trouble. Outnumbered and overpowered by the blacks, the white men jumped off the train.

Questioning the reason for his New York trip, the Morgan County solicitor asked, "Did you meet with Governor Franklin D. Roosevelt?"

Carter claimed the visit was "to clear his conscious." (In 1933, Roosevelt would become the 32nd President of the United States.)

"Did Brodsky buy the suit you have on? Who paid for your room and board?" questioned the prosecutor. "Yes sir," Carter responded. [23]

Next, E. L. Lewis, a black man and friend of Dallas Ramsey, corroborated Ramsey's statement. He informed the court that he had also seen Victoria Price in the hobo jungle before she left Chattanooga. The woman was in the company of several men, both white and black. Identifying Mrs. Price as the older of the women with dark hair, Lewis said that Price frequented the hobo jungle previously. On occasion, she stopped at his house and "asked his wife for food."[24]

Under cross-examination, Lewis said that before the women boarded the train, Lester Carter approached him with his hand in his pocket. Angry, he asked, "What did you say to them girls?"

"What girls?" asked Lewis.

"Them two white girls," retorted Carter, in a confrontational manner.[25]

Price had falsely claimed that the black man had been inappropriate with them. Lewis explained that he had said nothing to the women, adding that his friend had only told them what time the train was leaving.

During the trial, tensions continued to escalate throughout the city. That Wednesday afternoon, as Lewis left the County Courthouse, he was confronted by white men who threatened, "cursed and insulted" him. In broad daylight, a fiery cross was set ablaze near the Train Depot. Too afraid to board the train back to Chattanooga, Lewis hid himself until around two o'clock the next morning, when he was finally able to get on the train.[26]

A week and a half later, while Lewis was back in Decatur, his house burned to the ground. A short time afterward, he died mysteriously. Many believed that he was poisoned because of his testimony in Patterson's case. A Tennessee death certificate revealed that the cause of death was "Cerebral Hemorrhage."

On Thursday afternoon, an unexpected twist came when the lead defense counsel seemed to rest his case. After asking the judge for a short recess, he then called the name of his next witness. Everyone was stunned. Judge Horton rose from his bench and stood; for a moment there was total silence. And then a burst of rustling whispers swept the space like a thick fog. "All eyes were on the courtroom doors," described The *Decatur Daily*. Suddenly, there was a piercing creak as the heavy door swung open. When Ruby Bates, one of the accusers, emerged as the defense star witness, spectators in the courtroom gasped. Missing since February 27, many wondered about her whereabouts.

Appearing with Bates was a short, stocky woman, Mrs. May Jones. After being sworn in, she informed the court that she had brought the witness to trial at the request of the Rector of Advent Episcopal church in Birmingham.[27]

Following her, the fashionably dressed Ruby Bates strolled slowly toward the witness box. She sported a gray coat and her chestnut-brown hair was covered with a matching gray hat, and dark colored shoes. Stepping up on the wooden platform, she sat down and was sworn in.

The courtroom was quiet. Leibowitz began his questioning; he first established that he had never met

Bates before. Next, he ordered, "Bring out Victoria Price please." As Price promenaded into the courtroom, the two women glared at one another with an unflinching gaze. Ms. Bates pointed her finger in the direction of her hobo friend and identified Victoria as her traveling companion.[28] Showing her repulsion, Price's face mottled with fury. "Keep your temper," cautioned Knight.[29]

Bates testified that they had known one another for about two and a half years. The women worked together at the Margaret Mill. She said that her first encounter with Lester Carter and Jack Tiller was when she and Victoria Price went to see them on a chain gang. The prisoners had been working on a Huntsville road crew. Following their release from jail, the men stopped by the mill to see them. Much like Carter's story, Bates said that the next evening the foursome walked up Pulaski Pike to a Huntsville hobo jungle and had dealings together in some bushes. As the night went on, droplets of rain begin to fall. They moved to a box car, where they spent the night, indulging in more intimate behavior.[30]

After briefly recapping their movements the night before, Bates said she, Price and Carter hopped a freight train and headed for Chattanooga the next day. They left Jack Tiller, Ms. Price's boyfriend, behind. Upon arriving in Tennessee, "Carolina Slim," another hobo, joined them.

"Did you spend the night at Callie Brochie's?" Leibowitz asked.

Bates replied, "No sir," contradicting Victoria Price's earlier testimony and her previous statement at Scottsboro. She further admitted that she, Gilley, Carter, and Price spent the night at a place called "Hobo Swamp," near the railroad yards.[31] Since they could not find work, they jumped on the freight train traveling back to Alabama the next morning. Bates went on to describe the fight, saying that the blacks put all the white boys off the train—except Orville Gilley.

While Bates was under direct examination, Leibowitz pointed out inconsistencies in her initial testimony two years earlier at Jackson County. "You testified at Scottsboro that six negroes raped you and six negroes raped her, and one had a knife on your throat...who coached you to say that?" he asked.

Speaking louder than before, Bates made it clear that she had perjured herself previously. She denied being assaulted and stated that as far as she knew, Price hadn't been either.[32]

> *Question*: "What happened, did the negroes come in that car where you were?"
> *Answer*: "Not that I know of."
> *Question*: "Did any negro attack you that day?"
> *Answer*: "Not that I know of."
> *Question*: "Did any negro attack Victoria Price that day?"
> *Answer*: "No Sir."[33]

Ruby later identified a knife that her traveling companion had been carrying. She said that it was given to a deputy after they arrived at the Scottsboro jail.

When Patterson's attorney asked why she changed her story, Bates ascribed the discrepancies to what Victoria Price coerced her to say. "She told it and I told it just like she told it," she admitted. Expressing her fear of being arrested for prostitution, she testified that Victoria warned: "If I didn't say it, they would put us in jail."[34] Her story and Lester Carter's were very much alike. On cross examination, Attorney General Knight hit hard. "Where did you get that coat, hat and shoes?" he charged.

Bates answered "Well I bought it."

Again and again, he asked her where the money came from. At last she said, "I don't know." She finally confessed that the Rev. Dr. Harry Emerson Fosdick, Pastor of Riverside Church in New York had given her money to purchase the coat and hat. The shoes were not new; she said she had them for some while. Disturbed about the lies she had told previously and the fact that innocent boys would die in the electric chair, Bates said that the Northern preacher convinced her that telling the truth was the right thing to do.[35]

Practically badgering the witness, Knight asked, "Did you see a fight on the train?...Tell me whether or not you have syphilis or had syphilis?...Was the defendant one of them or not, did you see him with a pistol?" So as to intimidate the once State witness, he pressed even more aggressively. "Which is the truth, the story you told in Scottsboro, or the story you told now?" Appearing a bit rattled, Ruby Bates would often confess. "I told that at Scottsboro because Victoria told it" or "I said it but Victoria told me to."[36]

Unrelenting, Knight pushed harder, producing a letter Bates wrote to her boyfriend, Earl Streetman in January 1932. In it, she denied having been raped. Ruby did not shrink back at the underlying harshness in the prosecutor's voice. Her manner conveyed that she was now truthful about the rape. She also told of a previous meeting with the prosecutor and Victoria Price, where she refuted the rape allegation.

Later, the state recalled Ms. Bates and resumed

questioning her about her clothing, alluding that they were purchased by the Communists. The defense counsel objected and moved for a mistrial. The judge overruled the objection.

Racial tensions intensified following Bates' startling testimony in which she asserted that neither she nor her traveling companion, Victoria Price, had been attacked. That evening, after hearing that a mob organized in Huntsville and was headed to Decatur, Captain Joseph Burleson with the National Guard ordered the old Keller draw bridge over the Tennessee River at Decatur to remain open, holding back the threat of violence. Nine guardsmen with riot guns were immediately ordered to the Cornelian Hotel to protect the defense attorneys and witnesses, cited a *New York Times* reporter. Just before midnight, deputies and guardsmen moved Ruby Bates to a secret location. A detail was dispatched to thwart an alleged mob. [37]

Six hours were given for closing arguments, three for each side. H. G. Bailey was the first to speak for the state. He began with remarks about the fashionable New York clothes worn by Lester Carter and Ruby Bates. The second prosecutor to deliver closing arguments was Morgan County Solicitor Wade Wright. During a forceful and hostile summation, he played on the emotions of the courtroom, hooking his audience with deep seated racial hatred, white privilege, and bigotry.

"Did you ever hear of a more damnable effort to destroy and break down this girl? How did they do it?" Wright sneered. Openly ridiculing Lester Carter and labeling him as "Carterinsky," the County Solicitor bellowed, "That man Carter is a new kind of a man to me. Did you watch his hands? If he had been with Brodsky another two weeks he would have been down here with a pack on his back a-trying to sell you goods (referencing their anti-Semitism). Are you going to countenance that sort of thing?" A resounding "No!" parroted from courtroom observers. Raising questions as to where Carter and Bates got their clothing and who paid their rent while they were in New York, Wade Wright woofed. "Don't you know these people, these defense witnesses, are bought and paid for?...May the Lord have mercy on the soul of Ruby Bates!"[38]

Wright's speech aroused the dark consciousness of members of the jury and most of the courtroom spectators. Turning to the defense table, furiously, pointing his finger, he said: "Show them. Show them that Alabama justice cannot be bought with Jew money," reported *The New York Times*. At that slur, Leibowitz leapt up and demanded a mistrial. The judge quickly countered, denying the motion. Picking up where he left off, the prosecutor's voice rang louder, and a feverish burst of rage overtook the anxious crowd, "It was Brodsky, too, who brought in Ruby Bates. The same Brodsky who put the fancy city clothes, New York clothes, on Lester Carter, and I tell you, gentlemen, that Ruby Bates was guilty of perjury right here in this court room." At the end of Wright's hour-long delivery he declared that only a "guilty verdict" would demonstrate a victory.[39]

Judge Horton admonished the jurors to disregard the comment about "Jew Money from New York."[40]

Knight requested a recess. The jury was taken outside for a walk around the block.[41]

Late Thursday afternoon, Leibowitz stood eyeing the courtroom spectators. He began his closing address with a plea for a fair trial, as "The whole world is looking." "I shall appeal to your reason as logical, intelligent human beings, determined to give even this poor scrap of colored humanity a fair, square deal." His voice rose as he directed the jurors' attention to Wright's "hangman's speech." "What he is saying is, 'come on boys! We can lick this Jew from New York! Stick it into him! We're among our home folk.'" In a striking comment about Flanders Fields (World War I battlefields) Leibowitz reminded the jurors that race and ethnicities were not a factor. And, that no matter what, all men of all backgrounds braved the horrors of war and fought and died together and served their country. He advised the court that he was not receiving any fees for his services, not even expenses for him and his spouse. Mrs. Leibowitz accompanied him to Decatur. The chief defense attorney asserted:

> I'm interested solely in seeing that that poor moronic colored boy over there and his co-defendants in the other cases get a square shake of the dice, because I believe, before God, they are the victims of a dastardly frame-up. Mobs mean nothing to me. Let them take me out and hang me. My mission will have been served if I get these unfortunates the same justice that I would seek to achieve for any of you gentlemen if you came to New York and were unjustly accused.[42]

For over an hour and a half counsel for the defense argued brilliantly. Court adjourned for the evening.

The next day around 8:30 in the morning, Leibowitz picked up again. For nearly two hours straight, he stressed that there was a frame-up and pointed out that the defendant deserved a fair trial. Referring to the fight he said, "There would be no Scottsboro case if it had not been for the stupidity of the negro and the white hoboes." He further argued that the State never attempted to put Orville Gilley on the stand, even though he was with the two women at the time of the alleged rape.[43]

As he argued vigorously for his client's life, *The New York Times* conveyed that the chief defense attorney was near exhaustion and often stopped for a drink of water during his closing statement. In an attempt to convince the jury against a legal lynching, he rationalized, "If I cannot convince you through reasons of his innocence, take him and put him in the chair. But if he is innocent, don't send his crisp and burned body back to his mother." Leibowitz ended his lengthy argument by reciting the Lord's Prayer.

Following him, George Chamlee, echoed the same sentiment, with a plea to free Patterson, "Justice must be done. Don't crucify justice on the cross of race."[44]

All day long, telegraph couriers scurried in and out of the courtroom with messages for the judge and attorneys for both sides. Some of the communications asked for acquittals while others demanded the death penalty.

In his final closing remarks, State Prosecutor Knight stood and in a piercing voice, sharply admonished the jury, "I do not want a verdict based on racial prejudice or a religious creed." Aroused, he appealed for a guilty decision "based on the merits of the case." In Knight's line of reasoning, he stressed, "…Gentlemen, there can be but one verdict, and that verdict is death – death in the electric chair for raping Victoria Price."

Resenting the manner in which Bates and Carter had been treated during their stay in New York; Knight said that Carter was the hobo talking with his hands (using hand gestures). And of Ruby Bates he declared, "Yes she sold out lock stock and barrel. For a coat and a hat and God knows what else." Offering a harsh charge he continued,

> If you acquit this Negro, put a garland of roses around his neck, give him a supper and send him to New York City. There let Dr. Harry Fosdick dress him up in a high hat and morning coat, gray striped trousers and spats.[45]

In his stalwart voice, Knight declared, "The State of Alabama has not framed that Negro... I don't have to have people come down here and tell me the right thing to do." Asserting that he was not a murderer, he said he would have dismissed the indictments if he thought the nine blacks were innocent. He claimed, "This is no framed prosecution. It is a framed defense."[46]

After rebuttals, Judge Horton charged the jury for nearly half an hour. "The law has a stern duty to perform, and when women of the underworld come before it, the jury must consider that fact." Alluding to the complainants' character, he reminded the jurors that it was up to them to assess the credibility of the accusers. "One is Ruby Bates who admitted on the witness stand in this trial that she had perjured herself in the other case." He further advised them to "consider the evidence, you may consider not only her lack of virtue as admitted by her here, but also that she contradicted her previous testimony."[47]

Next, Horton said of Victoria Price, the facts prove "that she also was a woman of easy virtue." Once again, he directed the jury panel to examine the evidence as he reminded the twelve men that Price had given "false testimonies" regarding her actions in Chattanooga. In addition, he noted that the state had not denied that the woman had been intimate with Jack Tiller in the hobo jungle.

Urging the jurors to set aside any prejudice and keep an open mind, the judge further stated, "Take the evidence, sift it out and find the truths and untruths and render your verdict." The court contended that many things about the case might trouble the jurors, but in the name of justice, he urged them to be fair. Expressing his disposition, he stated that he had done what he thought was right, regardless of any potential consequences that might arise.

Horton further warned the jurors to put any thoughts of color, race, and sectionalism out of their minds. "You are not trying whether or not the defendant is white or black. You are not trying lawyers; you are not trying State lines." Additionally, he surmised that the white and black races were to live together. "It seems that love has almost deserted the human bosom and hate has taken its place," he exclaimed. The judge reasoned that the men were there to decide whether or not Patterson took the women by force and against their will. Ending his instructions, the magistrate made an appeal to the twelve Southern gentlemen, "I want to see righteousness done and justice done, and we are going to uphold that name."[48] Concluding he admonished the jury, "Wrong dies and truth lasts, we should have faith in that." The case went to the jury at 12:45 on Saturday, April 8, 1933. Following lunch, they began weighing the evidence.

On Palm Sunday morning, after twenty two hours of deliberation, while most churches congregated for worship, Judge Horton was summoned at his home in nearby Athens. The jury had reached a verdict. Anticipating threats, the National Guard remained on high alert. The defendant Haywood Patterson was led into the courtroom by Captain Burleson and several of his men "with rifles ready." Describing the scene, a *New York Times* reporter told: "The guns of the two guards behind the Negro dug into his back.[49] The attorneys for both sides joined Sheriff Davis, the Circuit Court clerk, and others as they assembled in court. John Holland the court stenographer was standing by with his pad and pencil. Reporters were in their designated places. Standing off to himself, twirling his cap, was John the courthouse janitor. Other than the defendant, he was the sole black man in the room.[50] Everyone was on edge, as they waited nervously for the judge to come.

After about forty minutes, the lean six-foot jurist arrived, his face appearing somewhat weary from the long proceedings. "Let the jury come in," he announced. As each of the jurors filed in from the small adjoining room where they had deliberated, some of the twelve men smiled as they gathered in front of Judge Horton. "Have you agreed on a verdict?"

Jury Foreman Eugene Bailey, Jr, carried a slip of paper in his hand and murmured, "We have your honor."

Handing the paper to Horton, the judge read, "We find the defendant guilty as charged and fix the punishment at death in the electric chair."[51]

Sitting stone-faced at the defense table, Haywood Patterson showed little emotion to the outside world.

The re-trial for Charlie Weems, the second of the Scottsboro nine, had been scheduled for April 17, 1933. Names of a hundred white men were pulled from the same jury pool as for the previous defendant, Haywood Patterson. Once again, Blacks were excluded from the jury roll. As the defense attorneys prepared for their case, a new level of racial animosity swept the River City and surrounding areas. The town that once prided itself on getting along with one another (as long as the blacks stayed in their place) was now filled with a haze of bitter anger and abhorrence. Judge Horton ordered a continuance "until such time when in its judgment a fair and impartial trial may be had."

Scottsboro defendants arrive in Decatur

Photo: Courtesy of Morgan County Archives

Joseph Brodsky, George Chamlee, Samuel Leibowitz
Photo: Courtesy of Morgan County Archives

Morgan County Courthouse scene
Photo: Courtesy of Morgan County Archives

Thomas Knight, Alabama Attorney General
Photo: Courtesy of Morgan County Archives

Scottsboro Defendants with Samuel Leibowitz *(seated),*
George Chamlee and Joseph Brodsky *(standing)*
Photo: Courtesy of Morgan County Archives

Morgan County Jurors and spectators in background
Photo: Courtesy of Morgan County Archives

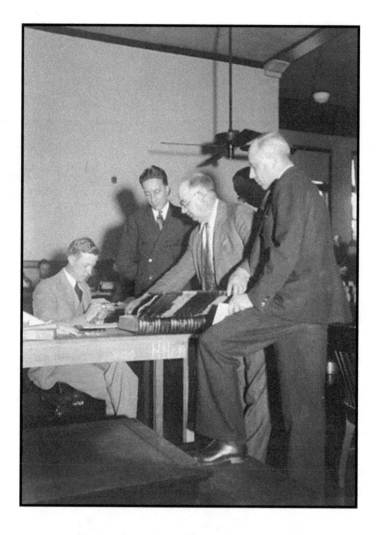

Examination of the Jury Roll
Thomas Knight, J. A. Tidwell and Samuel Leibowitz
Photo: Courtesy of Morgan County Archives

Crowded Corridor for Patterson
Trial at Morgan County
Photo: Courtesy of Morgan County Archives

Haywood Patterson with attorneys
Samuel Leibowitz (left) and George Chamlee (right)
Photo: Courtesy of Morgan County Archives

Victoria Price
Photo: Courtesy of Morgan County Archives

Ory Dobbins
Photo: Courtesy of Morgan County Archives

National Guard Morgan County Courthouse
Photo: Courtesy of Morgan County Archives

Haywood Patterson and mother Jane Patterson
Photo: Courtesy of Morgan County Archives

Dr. Robert R. Bridges, Judge James E. Horton looks on
Photo: Courtesy of Morgan County Archives

**P. Bernard Young, William Jones
and Haywood Patterson**
(Young and Jones: Black Press Reporters)
Photo: Courtesy of Morgan County Archives

**Jane Patterson, Beatrice Maddox, Ada Wright,
and unidentified female attending trial**
Photo: Courtesy of Morgan County Archives

Courtroom scene
Photo: Courtesy of Morgan County Archives

Percy Ricks
Train firemen
Photo: Courtesy of Morgan County Archives

Lester Carter
Photo: Courtesy of Morgan County Archives

Ruby Bates

(Recanted her story)

Photo: Courtesy of Morgan County Archives

Unidentified Witness
Photo: Courtesy of Morgan County Archives

Outside Courthouse Scene
Photo: Courtesy of Morgan County Archives

Thomas Brown
Photo: Courtesy of Morgan County Archives

CHAPTER 8

DÉJÀ VU

On the morning of June 22, 1933, Judge James E. Horton, Jr., left his home and traveled a block over to the Limestone County Courthouse. Climbing the steps, he opened the heavy wooden doors, took his seat behind the bench, and rapped his gavel for order. Horton began: *"Social Order is based on law, and its perpetuity on its fair and impartial administration. Deliberate justice is more fatal to the one who imposes it than to the one on whom it is imposed."*[1] Raising questions about the validity of the State's evidence and the reliability of witnesses' testimony, the Judge remarked, *"History, sacred and profane, and the common experience of mankind teach us that women of the character shown in this case are prone for selfish reasons to make false accusations both of rape and of insult."*[2] Further expounding on the evidence presented, he said it was clear that Victoria Price's testimony was not true. Outraged at his comments, Attorney General Knight's eyes were a smoldering glare. Reading his opinion for an hour or so, Judge Horton concluded:

> *The law declares that a defendant should not be convicted*
> *without corroboration where the testimony of prosecutrix*
> *bears on its face indications of unreliability or improbability*
> *and particularly when it is contradicted by other evidence*
> *and in addition thereto the evidence greatly preponderates*
> *in favor of the defendant...It is therefore ordered and*
> *adjudged by the Court that the motion be granted; that*
> *the verdict of the jury in this case and the judgment of the*
> *Court sentencing this defendant to death be set aside and*
> *that a new trial be and the same is hereby ordered.*[3]

Granting the defense motion, Horton reversed his previous decision and set aside the death sentence. For a second time, Haywood Patterson's life was spared the electric chair. Judge Horton received hundreds of letters from people all around the country, applauding him for his courage and willingness to take a stand for justice. While many commended him for this daring act of valor, others condemned his decisive decision, some with violent threats.

Charged by a hotbed of racial hatred, fueled with allegations of black men raping white women, outside interference and political ambition, the bombshell ruling was political suicide for Judge Horton. Subsequently, at the merciless insistence of Attorney General Knight, the remaining trials were moved from Horton's courtroom. Judge Horton lost his bid for re-election in June 1934.

On a warm summer morning in August 1933, a violent cyclone of fear dangerously whirled throughout Decatur. Tearfully, a white woman told how she was attacked with a "long bladed-knife" and dragged into a cornfield in broad daylight. The assault occurred in Enolam Oaks (between Seventh and Nineteenth Streets) around 11:30 a.m., near the old Wilder place.

Could this really be happening again, many wondered. In a town already embittered in searing hostility and terror, news of the alleged rape fueled further antagonism. Deputies and a citizen's posse had been organized, and a manhunt moved swiftly throughout every corner of East Town's black community. Following a tip, they quickly headed to Vine Street in Old Town. Abruptly, the wailing police sirens fell silent as several cars and trucks jerked to a squealing stop. Barreling out of their vehicles, with guns drawn and with the aid of barking bloodhounds, police flooded the neighborhood, carefully searching every inch of the area. Kicking in doors with little or no warning, the officers flicked on their flashlights as they rummaged every single clapboard house and business, searching under beds and in every corner. Moving in and out of old outhouses, they looked behind each bush and combed every street and alley.

Suddenly, a man bolted out of a back door, sprinting across an alley and up Sycamore Street. "Halt!" Audrey Watkins shouted. About the same time, a shot crackled through the hot, summer air. Thomas Brown (alias "Tom Brown" alias "Tom Jackson") stopped dead in his track. Sheriff deputies shoved him into a car and rushed him to Johnston Street City Hall.[4]

"That's him," the white woman said, hurriedly identifying her so-called attacker. Brown emphatically denied being in the vicinity. Throwing the prisoner into a squad car, the sheriff then transported him to the county jail. That evening, a crowd of more than 200 enraged men circled the jail in an attempt to lynch Brown. To circumvent the hanging, Sheriff Davis quickly pushed the prisoner into his car, slammed the gas pedal to the floor and bolted away. For safe keeping, the prisoner was carried to a secret location until the trial.[5]

After a failed lynching attempt, later that night James Royal, a sixteen-year-old medicine delivery boy, was killed. While Royal was not involved with assaulting Mrs. Minnie Dugger, he was targeted because he was black. A few days afterward, a group of about forty men went to the Madison County jail and made a second unsuccessful attempt to lynch Tom Brown.

Heightened anxieties generated fear. Patterson's trial had brought much dissension among the townsfolk. Now, rattled by the recent killing of James Royal and failed attempts to lynch Tom Brown, Decatur's black residents became increasingly uneasy. Many of them experienced acts of retribution because of the Scottsboro trial. They were afraid for their lives, property and livelihood.

The harrowing atrocities occurred only a few days before Charlie Weems' second trial was to begin. *The Decatur Daily* reported that Judge Horton postponed the trial on the grounds that he believed that chances of getting a fair trial would be impossible. Additionally, an account had been reported that Leibowitz had called the jurors "bigots."

Agents for the defense queried black citizens about Weems' upcoming trial. While some refused to discuss the case openly, others expressed their sentiments but did not want their name to be recorded. A few, however, did voice their opinions. For instance, Hannah Shelby, who lived at 701 Grove Street, attended Patterson's retrial in Decatur and felt there was a "lynch spirit right in and around the courtroom." She believed that the defendants could not get a fair trial in Decatur. Likewise, George Williams, of Walnut Street said that during the trial he heard one of the militiamen say, "Leibowitz and Ruby Bates ought to be killed." Susie Smith of Somerville Pike claimed to overhear one of the guardsman say, "The militia wouldn't protect the boys from lynching." Daisy Pitts had also gone to the trial and said, it was the worst frame-up. She believed that there would be trouble in Decatur if the trial was brought back to the city.[6]

Louise Johnson, 412 Cherry Street, acknowledged that "negro women couldn't get jobs in Decatur anymore." She knew of a particular case where a woman who worked at a hotel spoke favorably for the nine defendants, and she was fired immediately. Carnella Smith, from 416 Cherry Street remarked, "Why they just killed the Royal boy, and he was only 16 years old. They're lynching them here right now. What's the use talking about the Scottsboro boys getting a fair trial here?" Learlen Young said that the Scottsboro defendants couldn't get justice in the first trial in Decatur and they had no chance there again. Agreeing, a neighbor Mary Pickett said, "The day after the Royal boy was killed; the negroes couldn't even go to the jobs in the white sections."[7]

Henry Simmons conveyed that "if the case was heard in Decatur, there would be much bloodshed because of the lynch feeling." Rosie Kelley remarked, "The negroes are catching so much trouble now, if the case is tried here again, it will be too bad." E (Hiram) Hiter said that there would be trouble if the other trials were held in Decatur, "I hope to God my son never gets into such trouble, he said." Mary Prince of Pine Street pointed out that "Negroes were treated worst (*sic*) than ever before, since the last trial negroes have been losing their jobs and there was high feeling around Decatur against Negroes." During the Scottsboro trial, Elmira Whitiker's employer asked how she felt about the case. After sharing her honest opinion, she was laid off. Lily Matthews of Spruce Street believed that if the case was brought back to Decatur, "All us negroes will be chased around and given much trouble." Erlena Martin believed "mobs were being whipped up against the negroes and that if the case came up any further there would be lots of trouble because of the recent killing of Royal and the attempted lynching of Thomas Brown." Catherine Jones of Maple Street said, "It was a shame the way negroes are treated in Decatur."[8]

George (Georgia) Spraggins, of Third Avenue, said she was "afraid for her own boys to walk the streets because of the trouble around Decatur." Her neighbor, Jessie Jackson was quoted as saying that "He hoped the lawyers could get the case out of Decatur because all the negroes (*sic*) there were very much afraid of what would happen." According to E. Jones, who lived on that same street, "There wasn't a chance for fairness in Decatur...a negro boy of sixteen had been killed by a mob...without even having a charge against him. It would be ten times worst." He further stated that he "hoped to God the trial wouldn't come back."[9]

Robert Martin of Lafayette Street believed that the treatment of blacks was worst (*sic*) than it had ever been. The interviewer stated, Second Avenue resident Rosie Black said she was "afraid her own boys would be given trouble if the case came back to Decatur." Stephen Wind (Wynn) asserted "There wasn't a chance of getting a fair trial in Decatur…Mobs were being formed and a lynch sentiment was being whipped up in the vicinity." He added that, "Once they get started it wouldn't take but a few minutes to get the job over."[10]

Arriving from Huntsville, Tom Brown appeared for his arraignment. According to *The Decatur Daily*, Sheriff Davis and a group of fifty soldiers, and a force of about thirty Athens police officers escorted the prisoner back to Decatur. Judge Horton appointed attorneys Norman W. Harris, of Decatur and Jasper Newton (J.N.) Powell, Sr., of Hartselle, to represent the suspect. After a brief discussion, with their client, state solicitor Wade Wright read the indictment. The accused plead not guilty. Trial was set for the following Monday.

When court opened, September 4, 1933, one hundred guardsmen from Athens, Hartselle and Huntsville were on hand to protect the prisoner, as well as keep order. A local photographer, William A. Sullivan, was the first state witness to testify. He had been allowed in the jail to take pictures of the prisoner. The photo was entered as Exhibit A.

Next, Mrs. Dugger testified that when she passed a cornfield, around 11:30 that morning, a Negro with a knife approached her. During the attack, she said he threatened to slash her to pieces and warned that if she cried out, he would "cut my head off." After identifying Brown, she stated that the clothes he wore at the time of the arrest were similar to those of her attacker.[11] Several witnesses for the prosecution conspired to provide false statements about the alleged offender's whereabouts.

The defense prepared a detailed timeline of where Tom Brown was the morning of the alleged attack. First

Mary Brown, the respondent's mother, testified that she and her son had eaten breakfast together and that he left their northwest Lafayette Street home between six and seven. Decatur's City Sanitation Superintendent, James W. Pettey stated that he had seen Brown on Vine Street near Union Station (The Old Railroad Depot) between seven and seven thirty. He said it was a distance roughly of about 2 or 2 ½ miles from where the supposed attack occurred. Following him, Professor John H. Harris, a well-respected teacher, affirmed that he saw Brown on West Ninth Avenue between eight and nine o'clock. The next witness, George Vaughn, testified that he picked Brown up in his truck near the vicinity of Sykes Cemetery and dropped him off at Moulton Heights. That was between nine and ten. Sherman Allen, lived near the box factory, he testified that he had seen the accused at a barbecue stand in Moulton Heights. After him, Earl Williams, a white man who lived in Old Town on Sycamore Street, told the court that the defendant stopped by his furniture store about 11:50 that morning.[12] Moulton Heights was a distance of nearly five miles from the furniture store, making it impossible for Brown to be the accused.

Testifying in his own behalf, Brown denied all the charges, swearing that he was nowhere near the area on the morning Mrs. Dugger said she was attacked. He had gone to Moulton Heights and after returning to Old Town, stopped at Cornwell Café. The defendant was to meet a man there about purchasing a stove. While all the men ran when the heavily armed posse pounced on Old Town, Brown revealed that he was the only one fired upon. The cross-examination was volatile. The attorneys rested their case.

After a short time, a verdict was returned. "We the jury find the defendant guilty as charged in the indictment and fix the penalty as death. C. M. Mitchell, Foreman." The jury had spoken and Judge Callahan (magistrate of the Eighth Circuit Court) condemned Thomas Brown to electrocution. On October 1934, the Governor of Alabama commuted his sentence to life in prison. Brown was paroled for good behavior in 1943.

CHAPTER 9

DARKNESS IN THE DAYLIGHT

J ust before the Thanksgiving holiday, Patterson's third trial opened on November 20, 1933, Judge William Washington Callahan sat on the bench. A Lawrence County native, Callahan clerked in a law office and later sat for the bar. At seventy years old, the silver-haired man wore rimmed circled eyeglasses. The judge's flagrant abhorrent and disdainful attitude toward blacks was obvious.

Callahan's main objective was to "debunk the Scottsboro case," get the trial off the front pages of newspapers. Typewriters were banned from the courtroom. Cameras were forbidden inside and around the courthouse grounds. Specifically, instructing law officers to be on the watch, Judge Callahan snarled, "there ain't going to be no more 'picture snappin' round here."[1] He dismissed the National Guard and swore in several dozen sheriff's deputies to protect those associated with the cases, "defendants, lawyers and witnesses." When he assigned a three-day time limit for each trial, the judge earned the name, "Speedy Callahan."

He would preside over all the Scottsboro cases from the later part of 1933 to 1937. A reported racist and Klansman, he was cynical in his rulings, callous in his treatment of the defense witnesses, and frequently sided with the prosecutor.[2]

Seven of the defendants arrived in Decatur from the Birmingham jail around six in the morning. During the pre-trial, the legal teams and judge volleyed back and forth concerning motions to quash the indictments and to change the venue. Affidavits had been submitted by the defense to prove that the defendants could not receive a fair trial. Agents posing as door-to-door salesmen affirmed that hundreds of enraged white citizens openly expressed inherent feelings of racial hatred against the respondents, their lawyers' and others affiliated with the case.

Dismissing the jury, Callahan ordered Brodsky, counsel for the defense, to read the affidavits, suggesting that it was a public trial. Leibowitz protested, asserting that it would "aggravate an already inflamed public opinion."[3]

Brodsky began with the following comments from William D. Smith, the owner of Heavy's Lunch Room on Moulton Street. "There shouldn't be any trial for them damn niggers – 30 cents worth of rope would do the work and it wouldn't cost the county much." He went on to say, "...if the state don't kill them then the people here will." A bookkeeper at the Cotton Seed Press, Mr. John A. Lumas (Loomis) and his wife vented, "Those niggers should burn—if the state doesn't burn them then the people should take them out and lynch them, to teach the rest of the niggers a lesson." He further professed, "The people have made up their minds to take him (Leibowitz) and all the rest of the New York Jews and the 'niggers' and lynch them." Louis Argend, manager of American Café, agreed, "if there was another trial in Decatur, there would be a "neck-tie party." He vowed, "If those Jews come down here again, the people will lynch them and the niggers too."[4]

A local garage owner, Lawrence Frahn, expressed that no twelve men in the county would free the blacks— they needed to be hanged along with the Jews defending them. He declared that he "would burn them niggers if he could." One investigator said that John D. Wyker, owner of Wyker's Hardware store stated that the Negroes got a fair trial and there isn't any use spending a lots of money in retrying them. They should have strung them up when they caught them in Scottsboro. Repudiating the statement, Wyker swore that to the "best of his knowledge he had not made such a statement," and he believed that the defendants could get a fair trial in Decatur. Weighing in on the matter, Alvin L. Jolly surmised, the Jews were there to "make us let 'niggers' sit on our white jury but they will play (sic) hell doing it, for they may go out for a ride if they come here again." [5]

Some, like Lamar Moye, University of Alabama student at the time, said the Negroes should be tried in court and acquitted, since in his opinion they were innocent of the crime charged. In addition, he stated that there was a "mind to lynch" the black youth.[6] A Southern Railway car inspector, W. C. Campbell, said that he attended both trials and a "great bit of bitterness and hostility was expressed." He also stated that many people believed the defendants and their attorneys should be lynched and thrown in the Tennessee River. As well, former law enforcement officers believed that racial discriminatory opinions would jeopardize the accused due processed rights. For instance, Sheriff "Bud" Davis, deputy sheriff Edward R. Britnell, and policeman, William M. Simmons, all stated that they talked with people all over the county and that the defendants could not get a fair and impartial trial in Morgan County.

Numerous opinions were cited from people all over the county. The minute Brodsky finished reading the statements; the attorney general interrogated him about the list.

Next, Arthur Tidwell, Chairman of the Morgan County jury board took the stand. Assistant defense counsel Brodsky asked why J. J. Sykes' name had not appeared on the roll. Tidwell asserted "He was badly crippled…and there were other things."[7]

During the trial, while examining the 1931 Jackson County jury roll, Leibowitz discovered that names of blacks had been fraudulently placed on the rolls. They appeared either above or below the red lines that depicted the end of the rolls. The names of Hugh Sanford, Mark Taylor, K. D. Snodgrass, Pleas Larkin, Travis Mosley, and Cam Rudder were among those added in the book.

In light of this finding, Leibowitz offered Knight the opportunity to bring in any handwriting specialist of his choice. Knight declined. Subsequently, the lead attorney for the accused subpoenaed John V. Haring, a New York handwriting expert. Inspection of the jury rolls revealed that the names of black citizens had indeed, been inserted since the 1931 indictments.

Again, motions to quash the indictments and for a

change of venue were overruled. A third motion to appoint an official to take a statement from Ruby Bates was disposed of.[8]

Patterson's retrial opened with a not guilty plea. Upon entering the second floor courtroom, all spectators were searched for weapons, *The Decatur Daily* relayed. Blacks packed the section reserved for "Negroes." Outside the room of justice, armed deputies patrolled the hallway. Unlike the previous trials, Judge Callahan prohibited any loitering, therefore preventing onlookers from gathering in the corridor outside the courtroom.[9] What's more, Ruby Bates, the defense's chief witness, had been reported ill and in a New York hospital. Even so, the judge refused to delay the trial.

Under direct examination, Victoria Price once again gave vivid details of the alleged assault. As she finished her story, she turned toward Haywood Patterson, bobbed her head and pointed, "That defendant over there, Haywood Patterson, was one of them."[10] When Leibowitz finished questioning Ms. Price, he was exhausted and asked for a recess. Judge Callahan sneered, "Tomorrow, I think I will ask you to take a seat, so you won't get tired. You wore yourself out up and down the train."

Much of the same evidence as in earlier trials was offered. The differences were that Orville Gilley, the hobo who Patterson pulled back on the train was called to testify on behalf of the state. A self-proclaimed "wandering entertainer," Gilley was tall and had thick, black hair. He wore an old, much wrinkled, blue suit. While Gilley's account and that of Victoria Price's differed somewhat, he swore that Patterson assaulted both women. The witness disclosed that Attorney General Knight compensated him for his testimony. Direct examination by H. G. Bailey was short and lasted about sixteen minutes.

Leibowitz took over with a grueling cross-examination. Recapping the events on the train, Gilley spent nearly three hours on the witness stand. The defense asked if the state had purchased him any wearing apparels. Gilley answered that "the State hasn't bought me any clothes," but, that Knight had given him three dollars for a pair of shoes. He later added that the lead prosecutor sends his mother, who lived in Albertville, "a little money." Corroborating Bates' testimony, Gilley swore that he and the women did spend the night together in the jungle.[11]

Next, Sam Mitchell took the stand. A black farmhand who lived near Stevenson, he was the State's first and only black witness in the Scottsboro cases. Describing what he saw as the train passed by, he testified that there was a "mixed crowd" of blacks and whites on the moving locomotive. "They was rastlin' on a gondola car," he said. Under cross-examination, Mitchell testified that he had seen some "Negroes" in different cars from the engine to the caboose, but he couldn't recall seeing any women, confirming the defendant's account.[12]

The state then produced Luther Morris, who swore that from his barn he observed several black men pulling the screaming women back onto the moving train. When the lead attorney for the defense took over cross-examining Morris, he asked, "You came here to say you saw women?"

"That's improper," roared Callahan, "You must treat the witness with respect."

"I am," said Leibowitz.

Striking his gavel, Callahan shouted, "That's enough."[13]

When the attorney went to speak again, the judge said, "I have already said stop, you can have an exception."

After the skirmish of words ended, Patterson's defense then presented Morris with pictures from varying angles of the barn and railroad. The photographs had been taken by William A. Sullivan, a Decatur photographer, employed by the defense. Not only did Leibowitz prove that the witness was severely nearsighted and could not see from his farm to the track, but he also demonstrated that Morris could not see the photographs without the aid of eyeglasses, and that he was hard of hearing, too. Similarly, reducing the credibility of the attack, the testimonies of other witnesses contradicted one another.

All during the trial, while Patterson's attorneys questioned the witnesses, Judge Callahan repeatedly interrupted. Often, he sustained motions, before the state prosecutor did. Objections to the judge's actions were overruled. Again and again, Callahan banged his gavel, interjecting numerous warnings and sarcastic remarks into the proceedings such as, "Looks like Santa Clause has come here" and "That's enough of that, let's get on to something else." Trial spectators burst out in laughter at the judge's mockery. In one instance, when Leibowitz was questioning a state's witness, the judge cautioned, "something will happen if you don't stop."[14] When Callahan excluded certain testimony from previous trials, Leibowitz bristled and angrily demanded a mistrial. Once again, the motion was denied.

Four of Patterson's co-defendants took the stand in an effort to discredit Ms. Price's testimony, Willie Roberson, Ozie Powell, Olen Montgomery and Andy Wright. The defense asked each of the alleged suspects: "Did you see any women on the train?" All answered, "No Sir."

When Haywood Patterson took the stand, the attorney general read into the record testimony from the first trial. At one point Patterson boldly asserted, "I don't know what we said. We boys were scared. They told us if we don't confess they would kill us...and give us over to the mob." In an intense move, Patterson pointed toward H. G. Bailey and said that during the trial at Scottsboro, Bailey declared, "send them all to the electric chair, there are too many in the world anyway."[15]

The front page story of Lloyd Warner's lynching produced a chilling fear that gripped Decatur. A furious Missouri mob lynched Warner for raping a white girl. Using battering rams, they broke down the jail house door and dragged the prisoner out. A crowd of more than 7,000 onlookers (including women and children) watched as Warner was soaked in gasoline, hanged in an elm tree, and sat afire.[16]

As Patterson's trial drew to a close, the prosecutors made their closing summations. Wade Wright played on the Old South's conception using derogatory terms for blacks, such as Negress and Niggers, reported The *Afro American*. The ruthless chief prosecutor Knight urged the jurors, "You cannot avenge what has been done to Victoria Price, but you can prevent it from being done to another woman."

"I object," shouted Leibowitz, noting prejudice and passion.[17] Callahan overruled the motion.

During the defensive closing argument, Leibowitz stood, looked the jurors in the eyes and began his fervent plea. He described Knight's comments as an appeal for passion, and then begged the jury to weigh the evidence, as he reminded them of Lester Carter's and Orville Gilley's reputations. After directing their attention to Victoria Price's promiscuous character, Leibowitz posed the question: "How can you ever meet your Maker," when you have sent an innocent man to the electric chair?"[18]

Next, George Chamlee raised the point: "If this had been a white man, he wouldn't have been tried but once and maybe not at all."

The State prosecutor had the last word. As Thomas Knight closed, he shouted, "It is an appeal to passion."

Both sides rested, and before the jury retired for deliberation, Judge Callahan gave a lengthy charge. He announced that when a white woman makes a criminal complaint against a black man, "There is a very strong presumption that she did not yield voluntarily. Despite whether she was 'the most despised, ignorant, and abandoned woman of the community or the spotless virgin and daughter of a prominent home." Later, while explaining the penalties for a verdict, Callahan gave the jury three options, death in the electric chair, life in prison, or prison with a specific time frame. Rushing to the bench, Leibowitz and the prosecutor reminded the judge that he failed to properly instruct the jury because he had not included instructions for a possible acquittal.[19]

Callahan finished, "I overlooked one thing. I have given you the form for the verdict for the infliction of the death penalty or imprisonment. Of course, if the evidence fails to justify conviction, there oughtn't be any."[20]

While the panel deliberated Patterson's case, a jury for Clarence Norris was being selected.

The decision was swift, though. For a third time, twelve

white men convicted and sentenced both Patterson and Norris to die in the electric chair. Immediately, Leibowitz asked that the sentences be set aside. The remaining trials were postponed.

In light of the rape accusation involving Thomas Brown, the black community was engulfed in a raging inferno of uneasiness, fear and panic. Admitting his concern, The Reverend Eugene Mixon, pastor of King's Memorial Methodist Church, said he feared mob violence.[21] The Sunday morning after Thanksgiving, the Reverend B. Wesley Duvall invited Samuel Leibowitz, to speak at Shiloh Baptist Church, located on the corner of Lafayette and Alabama Street (6th Avenue). According to *The Afro American*, the lead defense counsel told the congregation that he had been "praying for justice."[22]

Two years later, the United States Supreme Court in *Norris vs Alabama*, negated the death sentences on the ground that there was systematic exclusion of blacks from jury rolls. As a result of the decision, the names of blacks would be included on Alabama's jury list.

Adhering to the recent federal court ruling, on November 13, 1935, Creed Conyers was the first black man to sit on an Alabama jury in 60 years, *The New York Time* conveyed.[15] A farmer from Paint Rock, Alabama, and

---

[15] "Whenever, by any action of a State, whether through its legislature, through its courts, or through its executive or administrative officers, all persons of the African race are excluded solely because of their race or color, from serving as grand jurors in the criminal prosecution of a person of the African race, the equal protection of the laws is denied to him, contrary to the Fourteenth Amendment of the Constitution of the United States. Strauder v. West Virginia, 100 U. S. 303; Neal v. Delaware, 103 U. S. 370, 103 U. S. 397; Gibson v. Mississippi, 162 U. S. 565." (JUSTIA US Supreme Court 2017)

the chairman of the Board of Trustees of Negro Schools, Conyers was on the Jackson County grand jury that issued re-indictments for the defendants.[23] Another black man, Bird Hill, of Bridgeport had also been drawn for the grand jury. He was 74 years old and excused because of his age.[24]

The first petit jury to include men of color was the one impaneled in 1867 to try Jefferson Davis for treason. That jury consisted of an equal number of white and black men.[25] (During the War of Rebellion, commonly known as the Civil War, Davis had been elected as the first and only Confederate president.)

CHAPTER 10

DROPPED CHARGES

By the time the Scottsboro defendant's appeals resumed in January 1936, they had been in prison for five years. Attorney Charles Watts, from Huntsville, Alabama, had joined Leibowitz's legal team. Taking the lead in arguing the cases, the Southern lawyer contended that the trials should be moved to federal court. Thomas Knight was now the newly elected Lieutenant Governor of the great state of Alabama. Watts challenged Knight's prosecuting the case, proposing that it was against the constitution, "To hold two offices of profit at the same time."[1] Judge Callahan denied the motion.

When Haywood Patterson's fourth trial opened, a winter storm severely crippled north Alabama. The hard-packed snow and ice-coated roads delayed the arrival of the Scottsboro defendants from Birmingham to Decatur.

A new day dawned in Alabama. For the first time since Reconstruction, the names of twelve Black citizens were included on Morgan County's 100-member panel of prospective jurors. Nonetheless, segregation was still evident, and when each group of twelve men was called, only white talesmen (person summoned to act as a juror) were permitted to sit in the jury box. Designated chairs had been arranged in a nearby area for blacks. Once, when a black man attempted to sit in the jury box, Judge Callahan pointed and bellowed with a menacing voice, "Here boy, sit over there." Even though blacks were now included on the jury roll, all were dismissed for one reason or the other.[2] Once more, Patterson's life would be in the hands of an all-white jury. An article in a newspaper later reported that the names of thirty-seven blacks had been included on a death list. A clear warning, that if blacks sat on the jury there would be consequences.[3]

Meanwhile, as the impaneled jurors considered Patterson's case, sixty-five men were drawn as potential jurors for Clarence Norris's trial. *The Decatur Daily* wrote that seven blacks had been excused, because they were all opposed to the death penalty. Among them were a teacher, a doctor, and Barry (Berry) Fogg, a World War I veteran. George Etheridge and two others were exempt because they were over age 65. Henry Mathison (Mattison) was asked "if he contributed to the Scottsboro defense fund," but after answering "no," he too, was dismissed.[4]

The trial proceeded quickly with much of the same evidence being presented. Melvin Hutson replaced Wade Wright and was ferocious in examining Patterson. Hutson was a Salem, Kentucky, native, who had relocated to Alabama. He was admitted to the bar in 1906 and appointed as solicitor of the Eighth Judicial Circuit in 1934. He would later become president of Mutual Savings and was known for bringing the company out of "insolvency and to a multi-million dollar success."[5]

Every so often, as the defendant was answering a question, Hutson would boorishly cut in with another question. During his summation, he cautioned the jurors that the womanhood of Alabama was looking to them for protection. "Say to yourselves," he implored, 'We're tired of this job' and put it behind you. Get it done quick and protect the fair womanhood of this great State."[6]

The defendant's attorney, Charles Watts appealed to the jury, "It takes courage to do the right thing in the face of public clamor for the wrong thing, but when justice is not administered fairly, governments disintegrate and there is no protection for anyone, man or woman, black or white."[7]

Convinced of Patterson's innocence, the jury foreman, John Burleson persuaded the jury to return a sentence less than death. When the twelve men returned to the courtroom, Burleson handed over a piece of paper with the verdict.[8] The defendant stood before the Judge for sentencing. When asked if he had anything to say, Patterson said, "Yes your honor, I am not guilty and I do not think justice has been done." His punishment was seventy-five years in prison. The sentence was suspended and the other trials postponed, until their appeal was heard.[9]

The town buzzed with horrifying reports. A sheriff's deputy, Edgar "Ed" Blalock, had been attacked with a knife by one of the Scottsboro defendants. The assaults happened while a caravan was returning the prisoners to the Birmingham jail. Sheriff Jonathan Street Sandlin, who accompanied Blalock in one of the cars, said he saw Powell brandishing a knife; he slammed his brakes, got out of the car and shot Powell. Handcuffed to Powell, Roy Wright and Clarence Norris were also in the vehicle. The prisoners told their attorney that the sheriff and his deputy taunted them while traveling back to Birmingham. When Powell dared to answer back, the deputy struck him, and Powell defended himself. Blalock received a minor laceration on his neck and was taken to the nearest hospital in Cullman. With a gunshot wound to the head, Powell was carried to a Birmingham hospital, fifty miles away. That evening, Earnest Merriweather, a twenty-two-year-old black delivery man, was arrested at a barbecue stand on Vine Street. Sheriff Sandlin recalled that the delivery boy had recently brought a package to the jail. He believed that he smuggled the knife in to Powell, at that time. Merriweather denied the charge.[10]

Trials reconvened during the stifling-hot summer month of July 1937. Lead prosecuting attorney, Thomas Knight died a few months earlier and now his assistant, Thomas Lawson, was the chief State Prosecutor. As in the case of previous appeals, Clarence Norris was convicted and sentenced to death by electrocution at Kilby Prison. The sentence was suspended pending the appeal.

Following him, Andy Wright's trial commenced. Robert S. Bridgeforth, pool hall operator, who testified that blacks were qualified to serve as jurors, had been impaneled, but excused because he didn't believe in the death penalty.[11] A prison term of ninety-nine years was imposed on Wright, twenty-four years above the maximum sentence.

On July 24, 1937, Charlie Weems' verdict returned with a seventy-five year prison sentence. When Ozie Powell was brought into court, Lawson unexpectedly announced that the rape charges would be dropped and an indictment for "assault with intent to murder," was read. Pleading guilty to attacking Deputy Ed Blalock, Powell was given twenty years to be served in the state penitentiary.

In another surprising turn, the lead prosecutor approached the bench and entered *"noll prossed"* (Latin for "we shall no longer prosecute," a declaration made to the judge by a prosecutor in a criminal case). Declining to bring to trial, Lawson dropped the cases on four of the defendants. Secret negotiations for release of the prisoners had been initiated in December, when Knight visited Leibowitz in New York.

Immediately, Leibowitz rushed to the jail. Signaling for Olen Montgomery, Roy Wright, Eugene Williams and Willie Roberson, the four were released and hurried out of the jail and into a waiting car. A condition of their release was that they "leave the state, never to return again." Another automobile carrying Leibowitz and his assistant, William Richter, followed them. The two getaway vehicles were provided by Dr. Newman Sykes, manager of the Solomon (S.S.) Sykes funeral home on Bank Street.

Shortly after the four were freed, Dr. Allen Knight Chalmers, chairman of the Scottsboro Defense Committee, would appeal to the Alabama Parole Board to free the remaining five. The three-panel board denied his request.

The following year, on July 5, 1938, Governor Bibb Graves commuted Clarence Norris' death sentence to life in prison. In November of the same year, Graves refused to pardon the remaining five.

CHAPTER 11

DISCHARGED

"I've got no hard feelings against anyone. I'm not mad...If she's still living, I feel sorry for her because I don't guess she sleeps much at night," said Andy Wright. Wrongly convicted, Wright left Kilby penitentiary for the last time in June 1950; nineteen years after being pulled off the train at Paint Rock with $13.45 in his pocket. He was the last of the Scottsboro Nine to be released.[1]

Andy Wright had first been released on parole in January 1944. Under an arrangement with Foshee lumber mill, his parole officer (who received kickbacks) brought parolees to work at the mill. Poorly paid, the men's hourly wage was 35 cents, and it was mandatory that they reside on site and pay the required $7 boarding fee. Extra money was taken from their pay for insurance and washing.[2] Work conditions were physically demanding with long hours, and some of the probationers experienced cruelty at the hands of the bigoted foreman.

Fleeing the terrible conditions of the lumber mill, Wright went to Mobile to be with his wife and to seek better job opportunities (an action that automatically violated his parole). Sometime later, Edgar (E.D.) Nixon, president of the National Association for Advancement of Colored People (NAACP), approached Wright and persuaded him to return to Montgomery. Nixon appealed to the Pardons Board to allow Wright to change jobs, and they agreed, and reinstated his probation. The parole was rescinded in 1947, when he was arrested for reckless driving and driving without a license.[3]

Haywood Patterson escaped Kilby Prison in 1948 and fled to Detroit, Michigan, where he played a game of hide and seek from authorities. In June 1950, he was involved in a bar fight and killed a man. Alabama sent extradition papers to Detroit, but the Governor of Michigan, Gerhard (G.) Mennen Williams refused. On August 24, 1952, one year after going back to prison, for murder, Patterson died of cancer.

The many years in prison took a physical and emotional toll on the defendants. For example, Ozie Powell was never the same after being shot in the head. During his incarceration, he suffered continued abuse at the hands of prison guards. On one occasion, he was given sixteen lashes for refusing to work. Having pleaded guilty and sentenced to twenty years for attacking deputy Blalock, Powell had been paroled from Atmore prison, on June 6, 1946. He returned home to Georgia.

In 1943, Charles Weems, the oldest of the youth arrested in 1931, was released from Kilby prison. The twelve years of incarceration were brutal. He often complained about abuse from the prison guards. Once he was beaten and tear-gassed for reading. Exposure to the gas caused severe and permanent vision problems. Another time, he was mistakenly stabbed by a guard who thought he was Andy

Wright. Weems returned home to Georgia after being freed.

Finishing school and enlisting in the United States Army in November 1943, Leroy (Roy) Wright appeared to be making steps in the right direction, to climb out of the pit that Alabama put him in. A sad twist of fate occurred on August 16, 1959, Wright shot his wife and then took his own life.[4] He suspected his wife Kathleen of being unfaithful.

Clarence Norris had been released on parole at the same time as Wright. On April 29, 1944, three months after his discharge, he married Dora Lee Broadnax. Following several clashes with his employer about the dreadful work conditions at the mill, he left the job. His employer immediately contacted the penitentiary and told them that, "Norris wouldn't work." Within fifteen minutes, he was behind bars once more. He would not be eligible for parole for another two years.

After serving two years for parole violation, Norris was granted parole in 1946. "When I walked out of prison"…he said, "I knew as I would never return to this place again." Norris jumped parole, fled up north, and took the identity of his brother, Willie Norris.[5]

Despite being a fugitive in Alabama, Clarence Norris, at age 64, contacted the NAACP about assisting him with getting a pardon. When he did not hear from them, he took it upon himself to contact the state parole board and was told, "If we can catch you, you'll be behind those walls again."[6] Norris spent fifteen years in prison, five of which had been on death row. Subsequently, the NAACP launched a campaign to pardon the last surviving "Scottsboro Boys." A young Montgomery attorney, Donald

V. Watkins, was retained as Norris' counsel. Watkins met with the Governor's office and Norman Ussery, chairman of the Pardon and Parole Board. Ussery still wanted to prosecute Norris. In August 1976, Watkins presented the case to Alabama's attorney general, William Baxley, and called for a full pardon. In a political move that could have been costly, Baxley outlined Alabama's tragic denial of justice for the Scottsboro Nine in a letter to the Pardon and Parole Board:

> *In my opinion, after a thorough review of all aspects of the case of Clarence Norris...this individual never should have been charged with any offense against Ruby Bates or Victoria Price, and his repeated sentences of death and his 15 years spent incarcerated in Alabama prisons can only be termed tragic.*[7]

Again, Ussery's position was as long as Norris was a fugitive and there was an outstanding warrant against him, he could not consider a pardon.

In an effort to get a pardon for Norris, the NAACP joined forces with Alabama's Black Political Caucus, led by State Representative Alvin Holmes. A campaign was initiated to bombard Governor George Wallace's office with thousands of letters and phone calls. The Parole Board decided in a vote of two to one to drop the delinquent warrant and reinstate an unsupervised parole. In an unprecedented move, the board then voted unanimously and recommended that Governor George Wallace pardon Norris. The request was sent to the Governor to sign. In a notable historical event, on October 25, 1976, the governor granted the pardon for Clarence Norris.

Just thirteen years earlier, this same governor

avowed to the world, in his fiery 1963 inaugural speech, "segregation now...segregation tomorrow...segregation forever." Several months later, Governor Wallace stood in the University of Alabama's doors, blocking black students Vivian Malone and James Hood.

The Scottsboro Boys were victims of the worst forms of tyranny and injustice. Eighty-two years after the nine innocent young men were convicted of a crime that never happened; on April 22, 2013, in a bipartisan effort; Alabama unmasked one of its most heinous crimes. Governor Robert Bentley signed bills to posthumously pardon Haywood Patterson, Charles Weems and Andy Wright. Another bill exonerated the nine Scottsboro co-defendants. "The Scottsboro Boys have finally received justice," said Governor Bentley. "It's important to clear the names of the Scottsboro Boys."

CONCLUSION

Many Americans still have not heard of the Scottsboro trials, and the nine youth who were falsely accused, hastily convicted, and all but one of them sentenced to die in the electric chair. When I tell the story of these "martyrs of Southern justice," people are astonished that such heinous injustice is part of our nation's history. They are equally amazed to learn that from the Jim Crowism of Alabama's Court system, because of these nine victims of intolerance and bigotry, came two landmark U.S. Supreme Court rulings that changed America's judicial system. Specifically, *Powell vs Alabama* stipulated that citizens are entitled to effective legal counsel in all cases, and *Norris vs Alabama* established that omitting African Americans from jury rolls was illegal (requiring a jury of one's peers).

For decades, people of color have suffered and still experience unfairness in the criminal justice system. While America has experienced many changes, from slavery to Jim Crow Laws, from the Civil Rights movement to the present, the wheels of justice move slow when it comes to discrimination in this area. A sad and painful reality is that in the first quarter of the 21st century, many people do not see that history is repeating itself in a seemingly never-ending, recurring cycle. With an increase of recent racial profiling, police brutality by a select few, senseless murders under the "stand your ground" laws, false convictions and disparities in sentencing, not to mention, the lack of judicial process, such as the case of Kharon Davis. A black man who as of late 2017, has been in an Alabama jail for a decade without bail and without a trial. Justice, which should be blind, apparently is not.

When will America open her eyes to see beyond racial bias and other prejudices? When will she find the courage to stand up for justice? The time is now. Standing for moral principles will not always sit well with the establishment. However, the courageous acts and sacrifices of men like Judge James E. Horton and the fearless blacks who took on Alabama's jury system demonstrated to the world that ordinary citizens could change inequitable practices. People like Samuel Leibowitz and his dream team, Ruby Bates, Dr. Bridges, and so many others, who despite adverse repercussions, showed the world that if we are to overcome the cruelty of intolerances we must diligently embrace certain challenges with fearless heroism.

Today, penitentiaries are crowded with an overwhelming number of young men of color, and the issue is not because whites have not committed the same crimes. It's because rather than justice being blind, the system continues to look with prejudice on skin color, sentencing whites with lesser punishments than their black counterparts. A 2016 study published by the *Bureau of Justice Statistics* revealed that African Americans are incarcerated at 5.1 times the rates of whites, and Latinos 1.4 times the rate of whites. In Alabama, more than half the prison population is black. Perhaps America should ask herself the question, "What if. What if it was my child, my son or my daughter, would I be as reckless with this life?" Looking at the heart of our insensitivity toward one another is imperative. Our nation must unite and expose the deep-rooted wrongs that continue to 'steal, kill and destroy' our youth. We can no longer rob future generations with such callousness because of the color of a person's skin, or socio-economic inequities. We have a moral obligation and we can no longer ignore these systemic problems.

Silence is not an option. May we remember the words of Dr. Martin Luther King, Jr., "Injustice anywhere is a threat to justice everywhere." My hope is that the courage of these people will inspire us to join hands, move forward and confront the many issues that continue to encroach upon our country today. Never forget that we are people of great strength, great perseverance and great resilience.

NAMES OF POTENTIAL JURORS FROM THE FOUR LISTS

H. L. Murphy

Tom Garth

Walker Lipscomb

W. A. Mills

Hess Thompson

Parker McKelvy

C. B. Irwin

Will Irwin

A.L. Harris

J. J. Sykes

Robert Smith

R. L. Hunter

G. F. Robertson

Carl M. Sykes

George Reynolds

Oscar Witaker

H. J. Banks

T. M. McWilliams

A. O. Sheffey

E. E. Jones

R. L. Anderson

F. G. Dinkin

Will Steel

Elias Hatton

W. E. Binford

Mack Sexton

Nathan Washington

Neel Sykes, Sr.

T. W. Bridges

Julius Williams

John Love

Will Porter

George Nelson

Henry Brown

Robert Browder

James Johnson

William Frierson

Albert Ruffin

Robert Bridgeforth

W. W. Bough (Baugh)

Henry Jackson

Edmond White

Dan Matthews

Hilliard Tate

Allen Draper

Amos Russell

John Humphrey

Clifton Draper

Will Jennings

Oscar Jackson

Oscar Sharply

Claybourn Sharply

Byrd Sharply

Lee Bibb

Allen Davis

Tom Davis

Jeff Robinson

Will Townsend

Will Garth (Cedar Lake)

Will Garth (Decatur)

Richard Vaughn

Charlie Tony

Dave Garth

Elmer Garth

Isom McDaniel

R. C. Smith

E. J. Pryor

William Martin

Jim Skinner

Alex Matthews

Henry Mattison

Billie Baker

Will Montgomery

William Murphy

Leslie Luckett

William Johnson

Will Terry

Will Turner

Aninias McDonald

W. J. Wilson

Professor J. E. Pickett

Rev. Robert Fuller

Rev. J. I. McGahee

Rev. Dillard Williams

Cal Barnett

Charlie Vaughn

Charlie County

Matthew Macklin

John Perry

Tom White

Robert Dawson

Clarence Poke (Pope)

J. J. Sykes

Robert Sykes

Tom E. Reedus

Frank Ballentine

Will Rogers

Jerry Elliott

Mack Lewis

Leo Sykes

Banks Patterson

Asa Jones

J. N. Martin

Forest Settle

Sam Whitaker

Scipio Garth

Hill Bolden

Daniel Thomas

J. C. Carpenter
James Lyle
Frank Owens
Albert Donald
Dr. T. R. Boalware
W. J. Wood
Walker Lipscomb
Stanley Basham
J. H. Harris
William Craig
William James
Phillip Lightfoot
I. Z. Moore
Charlie Montgomery
Will Terry
Rev. L. R. Womack
Rev. John Watkins
Rev. W. A. Wilhite
Rev. Newby
Rev. George Eldridge
Rev. U. G. Draper
John Dillon
J. J. Jackson
Robert Jackson
Ed Owens
William Gee
Abe Long
Dr. Frank Sykes
Rev. E. Mison (Mixon)
Rev. Arthur Matthews
Professor Council Harris
H. Swift

Arthur Roberson
Sam Deemer
C.   V. Hill
John Chandler
W. L. Swoops
F. K. Vaughn
John W. Bates
J. H. Vaughn
Dallas Priest
Charles Brooks
Frank Owens
Alonzo Harris
Harry Johnson
James Hill
Solomon Young
A. W. Matthews
Rev. Pollard
Dr. W. H. Sherard
Rev. James Hyter
Robert Pates
Otis Johnson
Green Shelby
Ed Harris
William Matthews
Edmond White
James Shelby
Joe Washington
P. F. Ballentine, Sr.,
Otis Johnson
Rev. James Cater
James Neal
Professor P. C. Nick

Professor N.I. McDonald
Willie Mathews
Charlie Toney
Professor Breeding
Dr. N. E. Cashin
Dr. Newman Sykes
Dr. D. V. Darden
Thomas Eldridge
John Eldridge
Oliver Garth
Rev. Willie Wilson
Dr. W. J. Wood
Percy Johnson
Aron Orr
Clarence Bailey
Luther Straughter
J. A. Dean

INDEX

159

161

SOURCE NOTES

(ENDNOTES)

Introduction

[1] (Powell v Alabama 2017)
[2] (State of Alabama vs Haywood Patterson. Motion for new trial. 1933).
[3] (Perske 2005)

Chapter 1

[1] (Court move to bring accused to trial with least possible delay. Tom Brown is spirited away 1933)
[2] (Dobson 2014)
[3] (Bullets pepper drug store. Second attempt to seize Brown fails 1933)
[4] (State of Alabama vs Haywood Patterson. Motion for new trial. 1933)

Chapter 2

[1] (D. T. Carter, Scottsboro. A Tragedy of the American South 1997, 5)
[2] (Acker 2008, 55)

Chapter 3

[1] (D. T. Carter, Scottsboro. A Tragedy of the American South 1987, 5)
[2] (Miller 2009, 170)
[3] (Excerpts from the testimony of Victori Price 1995-2017)
[4] (Revolting in last degree. 1931, 8)
[5] (Ozie Powell, Willie Roberson, Andy Wright and Olen Montgomery. Petioners vs State of Alanbama 1932, 38)
[6] (D. O. Linder, Scottsboro Boys Trial 1931-1937 1995-2015)
[7] (D. T. Carter, Scottsboro. A Tragedy of the American South 1987, 46)

[8] (Kinhasa 2014, 9)

[9] (D. Carter 2007, 33)

[10] Ibid.

[11] (D. T. Carter, Scottsboro. A Tragedy of the American South 1987, 45)

[12] (New York Times 1931)

[13] (Ransdell 1931, 14)

[14] (Goodman 1994, 5)

[15] (K. M. Kinshasa 1997, 36)

[16] (D. T. Carter, Scottsboro. A Tragedy of the American South 1987, 19)

[17] (K. M. Kinshasa 2014, 25)

[18] (D. T. Carter, Scottsboro. A Tragedy of the American South 1997)

[19] (D. T. Carter, Scottsboro. A Tragedy of the American South 1987, 22)

[20] Ibid.

[21] (K. M. Kinshasa 1997, 40)

[22] (D. T. Carter, Scottsboro. A Tragedy of the American South 1987, 14)

[23] Ibid.

[24] (Scottsboro: The Shame of America 1936, 12)

[25] (Death sentenced pronounced on eight negroes 1931, 1,8)

Chapter 4

[1] (Vile 2003, 391-393)

[2] (Guard Ordered 1933, 2)

[3] (D. T. Carter, Scottsboro. A Tragedy of the American South 1987, 188)

[4] (Fight for Negroes opens in Alabama. Witness put on stand. 1933)

[5] (Davenport, Horton charaterizes telegrams received by court as baubles 1933)

[6] (Acker 2008, 44)

[7] (Davenport, Defense As for Jury List 1933, 1)

[8] (Plot thickens 1931)

[9] (Norris vs State of Alabama. United States Supreme Court 1934. Transcript of Record 1934, 92)

[10] Ibid. p. 100

[11] Ibid. p. 105

[12] Ibid. p. 115

[13] Ibid. p. 118

[14] (D. T. Carter, Scottsboro. A Tragedy of the American South 1987, 197)

[15] (Norris vs State of Alabama. United States Supreme Court 1934. Transcript of Record 1934, 119)

[16] (D. T. Carter, Scottsboro. A Tragedy of the American South 1987, 198)

[17] (B. P. Young 1933, 3)

[18] (Norris vs State of Alabama. United States Supreme Court 1934. Transcript of Record 1934, 127-132)

[19] Ibid. 135-146

[20] (Davenport, Defense As for Jury List 1933)

Chapter 5

[1] (Feldman 2008, 201)

[2] (Spivak 1933, 2)

[3] (Spies quiz Jones. Young looking for red connections. 1933, 2)

[4] (Davenport, Morgan Negroes may be called to tell of juror qualifications 1933, 1)

[5] (Norris vs State. Supreme Court of Alabama March 1934. Transcript of Record 1935, 429)

[6] (Davenport, Decatur Daily 1933)

[7] (Norris vs State. Supreme Court of Alabama March 1934. Transcript of Record 1935, 436)

[8] (B. Young 1933, 14)

[9] (Norris vs State. Supreme Court of Alabama March 1934. Transcript of Record 1935, 445- 446)

[10] Ibid.

[11] (Norris vs State. Supreme Court of Alabama March 1934. Transcript of Record 1935, 447)

[12] (Norris vs State. Supreme Court of Alabama March 1934. Transcript of Record 1935, 455)

[13] (W. Jones 1933, 4)

[14] (Norris vs State. Supreme Court of Alabama March 1934. Transcript of Record 1935, 459)

[15] (Norris vs State. Supreme Court of Alabama March 1934. Transcript of Record 1935, 462)

[16] (Norris vs State. Supreme Court of Alabama March 1934. Transcript of Record 1935, 464)

[17] (Norris vs State. Supreme Court of Alabama March 1934. Transcript of Record 1935, 466)

[18] (Norris vs State. Supreme Court of Alabama March 1934. Transcript of Record 1935, 471)

[19] (R. Daniell, Bailiffs isolate Scottsboro jury 1933)

[20] (R. F. Daniell, Background study of Scottsboro case. 1933, 2)

[21] (Davenport, Exchanges sharp as questons are fired. Motion against severance denied. 1933)

[22] (Negro youth is mysteriously slain. James Royal is shot down. 1933)

Chapter 6

[1] (W. N. Jones 1933)

[2] (Davenport, Cross examination by defense counsel goes into details of events 1933)

[3] (Sordid Details Featured Victoria Price Rape Story 1933)

[4] Ibid.

[5] (Excerpts from the testimony of Victoria Price n.d.)

[6] Ibid.

[7] (Feldman 2008, 231)

[8] (State of Alabama v Patterson Trial Transcript 1933, 14)

[9] Ibid.

[10] Ibid.

[11] (Davenport, Cross examination by defense counsel goes into details of events 1933, 1)

[12] Ibid.

[13] Ibid.

[14] Ibid.

[15] (State of Alabama v Patterson Trial Transcript 1933, 81)

[16] (Goodman 1994, 125)

[17] (Bullets pepper drug store. Second attempt to seize Brown fails 1933, 4)

[18] (Davenport, Cross examination by defense counsel goes into details of events 1933, 1)

[19] Ibid.

[20] (State of Alabama v Patterson Trial Transcript 1933, 72)

[21] Ibid.

[22] (State of Alabama v Patterson Trial Transcript 1933, 99)

[23] Ibid.

[24] (Let's get Leibowitz 1933)

[25] (State of Alabama v Patterson Trial Transcript 1933)

[26] (Excerpts from Testimony of Dr. R. R. Bridges n.d.)

[27] Ibid.

[28] (Davenport, Exception is taken by Defense Attorney to Prosecutor's action 1933)

[29] Ibid.

[30] (Excerpts from the testimony of Ory Dobbins n.d.)

[31] Ibid.

[32] Ibid.

[33] (Davenport, Exception is taken by Defense Attorney to Prosecutor's action 1933)

[34] (Excerpts from testimony of Artur Woodall n.d.)

[35] Ibid.

[36] Ibid.

[37] (State of Alabama v Patterson Trial Transcript 1933, 293)

[38] (R. F. Daniell 1933)

Chapter 7

[1] (State of Alabama v Patterson Trial Transcript 1933, 302)

[2] (Excerpts of Testimony of Dallas Ramsey 1999)

[3] Ibid.

[4] (State of Alabama v Patterson Trial Transcript 1933, 314-315)

[5] (State of Alabama v Patterson Trial Transcript 1933)

[6] (State of Alabama vs Haywood Patterson. Motion for new trial. 1933)

[7] (Excerpts from the testimony of George W. Chamlee 1999)

[8] (Davenport, Defendant denies testimony in previous trial 1933, 8)

[9] Ibid.

[10] (D. O. Linder 2017)

[11] (Norris vs State. Supreme Court of Alabama March 1934. Transcript of Record 1935, 355)

[12] Ibid.

[13] (State of Alabama v Patterson Trial Transcript 1933, 402-421)

[14] (State of Alabama v Patterson Trial Transcript 1933, 422)

[15] (State of Alabama v Patterson Trial Transcript 1933, 445-478)

[16] Ibid.

[17] (Excerpts from the testimony of Lester Carter 1999)

[18] Ibid.

[19] Ibid.

[20] (State of Alabama v Patterson Trial Transcript 1933, 573)

[21] (State of Alabama v Patterson Trial Transcript 1933), 598

[22] Ibid, 605

[23] Ibid, 629

[24] (State of Alabama v Patterson Trial Transcript 1933, 645)

[25] Ibid.

[26] (State of Alabama vs Haywood Patterson. Motion for new trial. 1933, 61)

[27] (Davenport, Lester Carter takes stand for defense in fight on girl's story. 1933)

[28] Ibid.

[29] (R. Daniell, Girl recants story 1933)

[30] (State of Alabama v Patterson Trial Transcript 1933, 666)

[31] (Excerpts from the testiony of Ruby Bates 1999)

[32] Ibid.

[33] Ibid.

[34] Ibid.

[35] Ibid.

[36] (D. T. Carter, Scottsboro. A Tragedy of the American South 1987, 233)

[37] (R. Daniell, Girl recants story 1933)

[38] (R. F. Daniell, New York attacked in Scottsboro trial 1933)

[39] Ibid.

[40] Ibid.

[41] (Sidelights on Trial 1933)

[42] (Scottsboro An American Tragedy 2017)

[43] (Davenport, Horton charaterizes telegrams received by court as baubles 1933)

[44] (B. P. Young 1933)

[45] (Scottsboro An American Tragedy 2017)

[46] Ibid.

[47] (Scottsboro An American Tragedy 2017)

[48] Ibid.

[49] (Danielle 1933)

[50] Ibid.

[51] Ibid.

Chapter 8

[1] (D. O. Linder, Profile of Judge James Horton, Jr. Scottsboro Judge 1995-2016, 22)

[2] Ibid., p. 23

[3] Ibid., p. 23-24

[4] (Court move to bring accused to trial with least possible delay. Tom Brown is spirited away 1933)

[5] Ibid.

[6] (Clarence Norris, Petitioner vs The State of Alalbama 1934, 246, 248, 249)

[7] Ibid. 246, 247,

[8] Ibid. 247, 248, 248, 249, 250

[9] Ibid. 253, 256

[10] Ibid. 254, 257

[11] (Mrs. Dugger says the defendant Negro who attacked her in field 1933)

[12] (Notice of Appeal stays execution of sentence to the chair 1933)

Chapter 9

[1] (Kinhasa 2014, 97-98)

[2] (K. M. Kinshasa 2014, 97)

[3] (R. F. Daniell 1933)

[4] (Clarence Norris, Petitioner vs State of Alabama 1934, 203, 204)

[5] Ibid. 204, 205

[6] Ibid. 232

[7] (Davenport, Judge Callahan rules defense fails to show "Exclusion for Color" 1933)

[8] (Davenport, New York expert on stand scans rolls 1933, 1, 4)

[9] (Davenport, Court seeks to speed the work of putting tests 1933, 1)

[10] (Davenport, Monday afternoon session 1933, 6)

[11] (Davenport, Afternoon court session 1933, 5)

[12] (Clarence Norris, Petitioner vs State of Alabama 1934, 560)

[13] (Davenport, Witness say they saw battle of boys on board southern freight train 1933, 1)

[14] (ALA. wont wait for Ruby to recover 1933, 4)

[15] (Bits of testimony from Scottsboro Boys' trial 1933, 7)

[16] (Seven thousand spectators see attacker slain 1933)

[17] (Davenport, State pleads for death or freedom for Negro; Mistrial motion denied 1933)

[18] (Sidelights on Scottsboro trial 1933)

[19] (R. F. Daniell, Scottsboro case given to the jury which is locked up 1933)

[20] (Bits of testimony from Scottsboro Boys' trial 1933, 7)

[21] (C. Mitchell 1933, 1)

[22] (Sidelights on Scottsboro trial 1933, 7)

[23] (R. F. Daniell, New indictments in Scottsboro case with Negro on jury 1935, 1)

[24] (Negro farmer 1 of 18 1935)

[25] (First mixed petit jury in history impanneled to try Jeff Davis 1936, 4)

Chapter 10

[1] (Davenport, Patterson to face jury in initial case 1933)

[2] (R. F. Daniell, Negro veniermen appear in Decatur 1936, 2)

[3] (C. Mitchell 1933)

[4] (Davenport, Norris trial started with jury picking 1933)

[5] (Obituaries 1968)

[6] (D. T. Carter, Scottsboro. A Tragedy of the American South 1987, 345)

[7] (R. F. Daniell, Scottsboro case goes to the jury 1936)

[8] (D. T. Carter, Scottsboro. A Tragedy of the American South 1987, 347)

[9] (Ozie Powell is riddled as he pulls knife on guard in supposed escape effort 1936)

[10] (Negro delivery boy denies he took weapon in jail 1936, 1, 2)

[11] (99 year term handed to Scottsboro youth 1937, 1)

Chapter 11

[1] (D. T. Carter, Scottsboro. A Tragedy of the American South 1987, 413)

[2] (Goodman 1994, 370)

[3] (D. T. Carter, Scottsboro. A Tragedy of the American South 1987, 373)

[4] (After Escaping Chair One of Scottsboro nine shoots wife, kills self n.d., 1)

[5] (K. M. Kinshasa 1997, 155, 164)

[6] Ibid. 165

[7] Ibid. 167

BIBLIOGRAPHY

JUSTIA US Supreme Court. 2017. https://supreme.justia.com/cases/federal/us/294/587/ case.html (accessed September 1, 2017).

Acker, James R. *Scottsboro and its legacy. The cases that challenged American legal and social justice* . Westport: Praeger Publishers, 2008.

Afro American . "ALA. wont wait for Ruby to recover." December 2, 1933: 4.

Afro American. "99 year term handed to Scottsboro youth." 1937: 1.

Afro American. "Bits of testimony from Scottsboro Boys' trial." December 2, 1933.

Afro American. "Sidelights on Scottsboro trial." December 1933.

Afro American. "Sordid details featured Victoria Price rape story." April 22, 1933: 23.

*After Escaping Chair One of Scottsboro nine shoots wife, kills self.*n.d.

Alabama Courier. "Death sentenced pronounced on eight negroes." April 16, 1931: 1,8.

Alabama Courier. "Plot thickens." April 30, 1931: 1.

Alabama Courier. "Revolting in last degree." April 2, 1931: 8.

Alabama Justice. "Milwaukee Sentinel." April 15, 1933: 1.

Carter, Dan. *Scottsboro (Revised edition). A Tragedy of the American South. With a New Introduction .* Louisiana: Louisiana State University Press, 2007.

Carter, Dan T. *Scottsboro. A Tragedy of the American South.* Baton Rouge: Louisiana State University Press, 1987.

—. *Scottsboro. A Tragedy of the American South.* Louisiana: Louisiana State University Press, 1997.

Cates, David. *Scottsboro Boys.* Minneapolis: ABDO Publishing Company, 2012.

Clarence Norris vs State of Alabama Transcript of Record. (United States Supreme Court, September 1935).

Clarence Norris, Petitioner vs State of Alabama. 534 (The Supreme Court, November 17, 1934).

Court moves to bring accused to trial with least possible delay. Tom Brown is spirited away by the sheriff to unannounce jail as crowds gather here. "Decatur Daily." August 22, 1933: 1.

Cross examination by defense counsel goes into details of event. "Decatur Daily." April 3, 1933: 1.

Cross examination by defense counsel goes into details of event. "Decatur Daily." April 3, 1933.

Daniell, Raymon F. "New venue change asked for Negroes." *New York Times*, November 1933.

Daniell, Raymond. "Bailiffs isolate Scottsboro jury." *New York Times*, April 2, 1933.

Daniell, Raymond F. "Negro veniermen appear in Decatur." *New York Times*, 1936: 2.

Daniell, Raymond F. "New indictments in Scottsboro case with Negro on jury." *New York Times*, November 1935: 1.

—. "Background study of Scottsboro case." *New York Times*, April 1933: 2.

—. "New York attacked in Scottsboro trial." *New York Times*, April 8, 1933: 30.

—. "Scottsboro case goes to the jury." *New York Times*, January 23, 1936.

Daniell, Raymond F. "Scottsboro case given to the jury which is locked up." *New York Times*, 1933: 1, 15.

Daniell, Raymond F. "Bailiffs isolate Scottsboro jury." *The New York Times*, April 2, 1933.

Daniell, Raymond. "Girl recants story." *New York Times*, April 7, 1933.

Danielle, Raymond F. "Negro found guilty in Scottsboro case; jury out for 22 hours." *New York Times*, April 10, 1933: 1.

Davenport, T. M. "Court seeks to speed the work of putting tests." *Decatur Daily*, November 1933: 1.

—. "Exchanges sharp as questons are fired. Motion against severance denied." *Decatur Daily*, March 30, 1933: 1.

—. "Morgan Negroes may be called to tell of juror qualifications." *Decatur Daily*, March 1933, 1933: 1-2.

—. *Decatur Daily*, April 1933: 1-2.

—. "Afternoon court session." *Decatur Daily*, November 29, 1933.

—. "Afternoon court session." *Decatur Daily*, November 29, 1933.

—. "Cross examination by defense counsel goes into details of events." *Decatur Daily*, April 3, 1933: 1.

—. "Defense As for Jury List." *Decatur Daily*, March 28, 1933: 1.

—. "Defense ask for jury list of Jackson County." *Decatur Daily*, April 1933: 1.

—. "Exception is taken by Defense Attorney to Prosecutor's action." *Decatur Daily*, April 4, 1933: 5.

—. "Horton charaterizes telegrams received by court as baubles." *Decatur Daily*, April 8, 1933: 1.

—. "Lester Carter takes stand for defense in fight on girl's story." *Decatur Daily*, April 6, 1933: 1.

—. "Monday afternoon session." *Decatur Daily*, November 29, 1933.

—. "Witness say they saw battle of boys on board southern freight train." *Decatur Daily*, November 28, 1933.

—. "Defendant denies testimony in previous trial." *Decatur*, April 6, 1933.

Davenport, T. M. "Judge Callahan rules defense fails to show "Exclusion for Color"." *Decatur Daily*, 1933: 1.

Davenport, T. M. "Judge Callahan to hear motion to quash venire Thursday; Trial speeded." *Decatur Daily*, 1933: 1.

—. "Decatur Daily." *Jury selected in long session*, April 1, 1933: 1.

Davenport, T. M. "New York expert on stand scans rolls." *Decatur Daily*, November 1933: 1, 4.

Davenport, T. M. "Norris trial started with jury picking." *Decatur Daily*, January 1933: 1.

Davenport, T. M. "Patterson to face jury in initial case." *Decatur Daily*, January 1933.

Davenport, T. M. "State pleads for death or freedom for Negro; Mistrial motion denied." *Decatur Daily*, November 1933: 1.

Davenport, T. M. "Witnesses say they saw battle of boys on Southern freight train." *Decatur Daily*, November 1933: 1.

Decatur Daily . "Obituaries." November 3, 1968.

Decatur Daily. "Bullets pepper drug store. Second attempt to seize Brown fails." August 23, 1933: 1.

Decatur Daily. "Court move to bring accused to trial with least possible delay. Tom Brown is spirited away." August 1933: 1.

Decatur Daily. "Defendant denies testimony given in previous trial." April 6, 1933: 8.

Decatur Daily. "Guard Ordered." April 1933: 2.

Decatur Daily. "Mrs. Dugger says the defendant Negro who attacked her in field." September 4, 1933.

Decatur Daily. "Negro youth is mysteriously slain. James Royal is shot down." August 22, 1933: 1.

Decatur Daily. "Notice of Appeal stays execution of sentence to the chair." September 5, 1933.

Decatur Daily. "Record of first trial introduced." April 4, 1933: 6.

Decatur Daily. "Seven thousand spectators see attacker slain." November 29, 1933.

Decatur Daily. "Sidelights on Trial." April 8, 1933: 1.

Defense ask for jury list of jackson county. "Decatur Daily."
    April 1933: 1.

Dobson, Celeste Sherard, interview by Peggy Allen Towns.
    (February 15, 2014).

Excerpts from testimony of Artur Woodall. n.d. http://law2.
    umkc.edu/faculty/projects/ftrials/scottsbor o/
    woodall.html (accessed July 17, 2016).

Excerpts from Testimony of Dr. R. R. Bridges. n.d. http://
    law2.umkc.edu/faculty/projects/ftrials/scottsbor
    o/SB_33Brid.html (accessed 5 10, 2016).

Excerpts from the testimony of Lester Carter. 1999. http://
    law2.umkc.edu/faculty/PROJECTS/FTRIALS/
    scotts boro/Cartertestimony.html (accessed May
    10, 2016).

Excerpts from the testimony of George W. Chamlee. 1999.
    http://law2.umkc.edu/faculty/projects/ftrials/
    scottsbor o/Chamleetestimony.html (accessed
    March 6, 2016).

Excerpts from the testimony of Ory Dobbins. n.d. http://law2.
    umkc.edu/faculty/projects/ftrials/scottsbor o/
    Dobbin_.html (accessed July 16, 2016).

Excerpts from the testimony of Victori Price. 1995-2017.
    http://ebooks.library.cornell.edu/s/scott/pdf/
    scott3016 .pdf (accessed July 15, 2015).

Excerpts from the testimony of Victoria Price. n.d. http://law2.umkc.edu/faculty/projects/ftrials/scottsboro/price.html (accessed June 15, 2016).

Excerpts from the testiony of Ruby Bates. 1999. http://law2.umkc.edu/faculty/projects/ftrials/scottsboro/Batestestimony.html (accessed January 29, 2016).

Excerpts of Testimony of Dallas Ramsey. 1999. http://law2.umkc.edu/faculty/projects/ftrials/scottsboro/Ramseytestimony.html (accessed January 29, 2016).

Feldman, Ellen. *Scottsboro. A Novel.* New York: WW Norton & Company, Inc., 2008.

"First mixed petit jury in history impanneled to try Jeff Davis." *Afro American,* February 1936: 4.

Good humored crowd mills in corridor as first session starts. "Decatur Daily." March 27, 1933: 1.

Goodman, James. *Stories of Scottsboro.* New York: Vintage, 1994.

Jones, William N. "The Afro American." *Reporting trial of Scottsboro trials has many thrills.,* April 22, 1933: 2.

Jones, William N. "Decatur lad's Ma crushed by verdict." *Afro American,* April 15, 1933: 14.

Jones, William. "The Afro American." *No spotlight for Scottsboro boys last week. Pastor school head speaks up.,* April 8, 1933: 4.

Jury board chief on stand an hour. "Associated Press." March 1933.

Kinhasa, Kwando M. *The Scottsboro boys in their own words. Selected letters, 1931-1950.* Jefferson: McFarland and Company, Inc., 2014.

Kinshasa, Kwando M. *The Scottsboro boys in their own words. Selected letters.* Jefferson: McFarland and Company, Inc., Publisher, 2014.

Kinshasa, Kwando M. *The Scottsboro Boys in Their Own Words: Selected Letters, 1931–1950.* Jefferson: McFarland & Company, Inc. Publishers, 2014.

Kinshasa, Kwando Mbiassi. *The man from Scottsboro.* Jefferson: McFarland and Company, Inc., 1997.

Lawyers for 9 Alabama Negroes "Warned". "New York Times." June 6, 1931.

Let's get Lebowitz. "The Afro American." April 15, 1933: 1.

Linder, Douglas O. *Famous Trials.* March 8, 2017. http://www.famous-trials.com/scottsboroboys/1586-robersontestimony (accessed March 8, 2017).

Linder, Douglas O. *Profile of Judge James Horton, Jr. Scottsboro Judge.* 1995-2016. http://www.law.umkc.edu/faculty/projects/FTrials/trial heroes/essayhorton.html (accessed December 21, 2016).

—. *Scottsboro Boys Trial 1931-1937.* 1995-2015. http://law2.umkc.edu/faculty/projects/ftrials/scottsbor o/

SB_bSBs.html#Roy%20Wright (accessed June 30, 2015).

Miller, James A. *Remembering Scottsboro. The legacy of an infamous trial.* New Jersey: Princeton University Press, 2009.

Mitchell, Clarence. "37 colored on Decatur death list of mob." *Afro American*, December 2, 1933.

Mitchell, Clarrence. "Bar Afro man from Decatur press table." *Afro American*, December 2, 1933.

"Negro delivery boy denies he took weapon in jail." *Decatur Daily*, January 1936.

"Negro farmer 1 of 18." *Decatur Daily*, November 1935.

New York Times . "Fight for Negroes opens in Alabama. Witness put on stand." March 28, 1933.

Norris vs State. Supreme Court of Alabama March 1934. Transcript of Record. (Supreme Court, November 1935).

"Ozie Powell is riddled as he pulls knife on guard in supposed escape effort." *Decatur Daily*, January 1936: 1.

Ozie Powell, Willie Roberson, Andy Wright and Olen Montgomery. Petioners vs State of Alanbama. 98 (The Supreme Court, October 1932).

Perske, Robert. "Mental Retardation." *Unlikely heroes,* 2005: 372.

Powell v Alabama. June 27, 2017. https://en.wikipedia.org/wiki/Powell_v._Alabama (accessed September 18, 2017).

Ransdell, Hollace. *Report of the Scottsboro, ALA case.* Report for American Civil Liberties Union, 1931.

"Reporting story of Scottsboro Case had many thrills, Jones tells Afro Club." *The Afro American,* 1933: 2.

Reynolds, Quentin. *Courtroom. The story of Samuel S. Lebowitz.* H. Wolff Book Manufacturing: New York, 1950.

SCLC defense mentally retarded man accussed of rape. "Jet Magazine." July 27, 1978: 6.

"Scottsboro An American Tragedy." *PBS. American Experience.* 2017. http://www.pbs.org/wgbh//amex/scottsboro/filmmore/ps_horton.html (accessed June 15, 2017).

Scottsboro: The Shame of America. New York: Scottsboro Defense Committee, 1936.

Sidelights on trial. "Decatur Daily." April 3, 1933: 1. Sorenson, Lita. *The Scottsboro boys trial. A primary source account.* New York: Rosen Publishing Group Inc., 2004.

Spivak, John L. "Bugs and ghost fill cell of Scottsboro boys." *The Afro American,* April 8, 1933: 14.

State Minutes . (Morgan Circuit Court, 1934-1943).

State of Alabama Jackson County Indictment. 2402 (Circuit Court of the NInth Judicial, April 6, 1931).

State of Alabama v Patterson Trial Transcript. (March 31, 1933).

State of Alabama vs Haywood Patterson. (Circuit of Morgan County, April 15, 1933).

State of Alabama vs Haywood Patterson. Motion for New Trial. (Circuit Court of Morgan County Alabama, April 15, 1933).

State of Alabama vs Haywood Patterson. Motion for new trial. (Circuit Court of Morgan County Alabama., April 15, 1933).

The Afro American . "One and one-half section for colored, four for whites." April 8, 1933: 3.

The Afro American. "Let's get Leibowitz." April 15, 1933.

The Afro American. "Sordid Details Featured Victoria Price Rape Story." April 22, 1933: 23.

The Afro American. "Spies quiz Jones. Young looking for red connections." April 8, 1933: 3.

Thompson-Miller, Ruth, Feagin, Joe, Picca, Leslie H. *Jim Crow's Legacy: The Lasting Impact of Segregation.* Lanham: Rowman and Littlefield, 2015.

Vile, John R (Editoro). *Great American Judges. An Encyclopedia, Volumn 1.* Santa Barbara: ABC-CLIO, Inc, 2003.

Wikipedia. 2013. https://en.wilkepedia.org/wki/ Jim_Crow_Laws (accessed June 30, 2015).

Young, Bernard P. "Onlookers sob as Leibowitz ends 3-hour plea." *Afro American,* April 15, 1933: 2.

Young, Bernard. "Defense ahead in Decatur trial now." *The Afro American,* April 8, 1933: 14.

Young, Bernard, P. "Even Scottsboro judge uses offensive language epithet applied to Negroes." *The Afro American,* April 8, 1933: 3.

ABOUT THE AUTHOR

Peggy **Allen Towns** is a local historian of African American history. She is a native of Decatur, Alabama, and her passion is preserving the voices and legacy of African Americans in her home town. She lectures and facilitates workshops on genealogy, local people and historical places. She is dedicated to identifying historic places, and as a result of her efforts, several sites have been listed on the Alabama Register of Landmarks and Heritage and the National Register of Historic Places. She has done extensive research documenting her family's history, which led to the discovery of a relative who served with the 110th United States Colored Infantry and the writing of her first book, *Duty Driven: The Plight of North Alabama's African Americans During the Civil War.*

CPSIA information can be obtained
at www.ICGtesting.com
Printed in the USA
BVHW08*0108300818
525864BV00001B/10/P

9 781546 225690